IMAGES
of America

HOPKINTON

I0799412

IMAGES
of America

HOPKINTON

Gordon E. Hopper

ARCADIA
PUBLISHING

Copyright © 1997 by Gordon E. Hopper
ISBN 978-0-7385-9014-1

Published by Arcadia Publishing
Charleston, South Carolina

Printed in the United States of America

For all general information contact Arcadia Publishing at:
Telephone 843-853-2070
Fax 843-853-0044
E-mail sales@arcadiapublishing.com
For customer service and orders:
Toll-Free 1-888-313-2665

Visit us on the Internet at www.arcadiapublishing.com

Contents

Acknowledgments

Many of the photographs used in this book were taken from private collections owned by residents of Hopkinton.

Some of the pictures were taken by the author, and several were supplied by two historical societies and the Hopkinton Fire Department. My good friends Isabel Smith and Norton Clark were major contributors to the collection used in this book.

Photographs were supplied by the Hopkinton Historical Society, the Ashland Historical Society, the Hopkinton Fire Department, Boston Edison Company, Ruth Ward, Sandra Cram, Isabel Smith, Norton Clark, Jack Beattie, Earl Cronin, Edward McManus, Russell Stratton, Catherine Smith, Roland Temple, Agnes Frieh, Robert D. Paquet, Frank Wylie Jr., and Vera Burns.

Introduction

Hopkinton is a small Massachusetts town located in the hills of the southwestern part of Middlesex County, 27 miles west of Boston. The town was incorporated in 1715, and its area includes more than 27 square miles. The highest point in Middlesex County is located within Hopkinton's boundaries. In 1909 the population was approximately 2,600 people; today it is approaching 11,000. A group of three mineral springs were used for healthful purposes about 150 years ago. Many people visited the site of these springs and stayed at a hotel located nearby. Ice House Pond, a small pond owned by the Town on West Main Street, is used for public skating during the winter months. The site now includes a small attractive gazebo.

Hopkinton was the birthplace of Captain Daniel Shay, the leader of Shay's Rebellion, and of John Young, the father of the noted Mormon leader, Brigham Young. Nathaniel "God" Smith, the leader of a small religious sect, lived on East Main Street during the 1800s, where he acted as the toll collector for the Central Turnpike. Major General Frank D. Merrill, the leader of "Merrill's Marauders" in World War II, was also born in Hopkinton.

There have been three major fires in the downtown section of Hopkinton. The first one on March 26, 1876, destroyed a large boot factory, a post office, a hotel, a church, and numerous other buildings located on the north side of Main Street. The second fire, which occurred on April 4, 1882, was a larger fire than the one six years earlier. It hurt the growth of Hopkinton, and it wiped out practically all of Hopkinton's business section. The Bridges & Co. factory, the mainstay of the town, was destroyed and six hundred jobs were lost. On March 15, 1900, the town hall and four business blocks were destroyed by another fire. This was approximately the same area that had been burned out in 1882.

Railroad service was provided between Milford, Hopkinton, and Ashland from 1872 until 1954, and streetcar service was provided between Hopkinton and Westboro, Milford and Framingham from 1896 to 1928. Bus service was provided for several years after the streetcars ceased their operation. Transportation for residents is now provided by LIFT buses and private automobiles. There is a heliport at the Tennessee Gas Pipeline complex on Wilson Street, but it does not provide a public service.

Hopkinton has many thriving businesses and a variety of enjoyable annual events. Privately owned granite quarries once operated at points on Lumber Street, Cedar Street, and Rafferty Road. A variety of industries are now located in the Hopkinton Industrial Park, a large area located on South Street. Route 495 provides an easy access to the industrial park. A second industrial area called Elmwood Industrial Park is being developed on Elm Street. The town is also served by Routes 85 and 135. An annual marathon run to Boston from Ashland was established in 1897, and its starting line was moved to Hopkinton twenty-seven years later. In 1997 the Boston Marathon celebrated its 100th running.

Residents today enjoy the town's strong school system, its lovely churches, excellent library, and wide range of recreational facilities. Hopkinton contains the sources of the Charles and Sudbury Rivers and its Mill River is a tributary of the Blackstone River. The town is also graced by the presence of Lake Maspenock, Echo Lake, Lake Whitehall, and the Hopkinton Reservoir. Echo Lake provides water for the nearby town of Milford. Public worship is conducted in several churches; the town has seven cemeteries, including one known as "the Tombs." Excellent education programs are provided by the Hopkinton school system. In the mid-1990s, a new middle school was initiated. A beautiful town common located in the center of Hopkinton includes the Veterans Memorial Gazebo, dedicated to Hopkinton veterans of all wars; it is used for memorial services and band concerts. Police and fire stations are located on Main Street, and a large addition is presently under construction at the fire station. Fire-fighting equipment is also kept at a second fire station located in the Woodville section of the town. The Hopkinton State Park, a large area operated by the state, is located off Cedar Street. The Hopkinton Public Library is a very attractive and well-arranged building containing a quite useful and enjoyable collection of books. Water of fine quality is supplied by the Town from a system of wells located on Fruit and Pond Streets, and the construction of a municipal sewer system is under way at the present time.

Hopkinton continues to grow. This is evidenced by the increasing number of schoolchildren. Several new schools are now in the planning stages. Many expensive homes have been built in the outlying sections of the town, and the two industrial areas are presently expanding.

One

Main Street

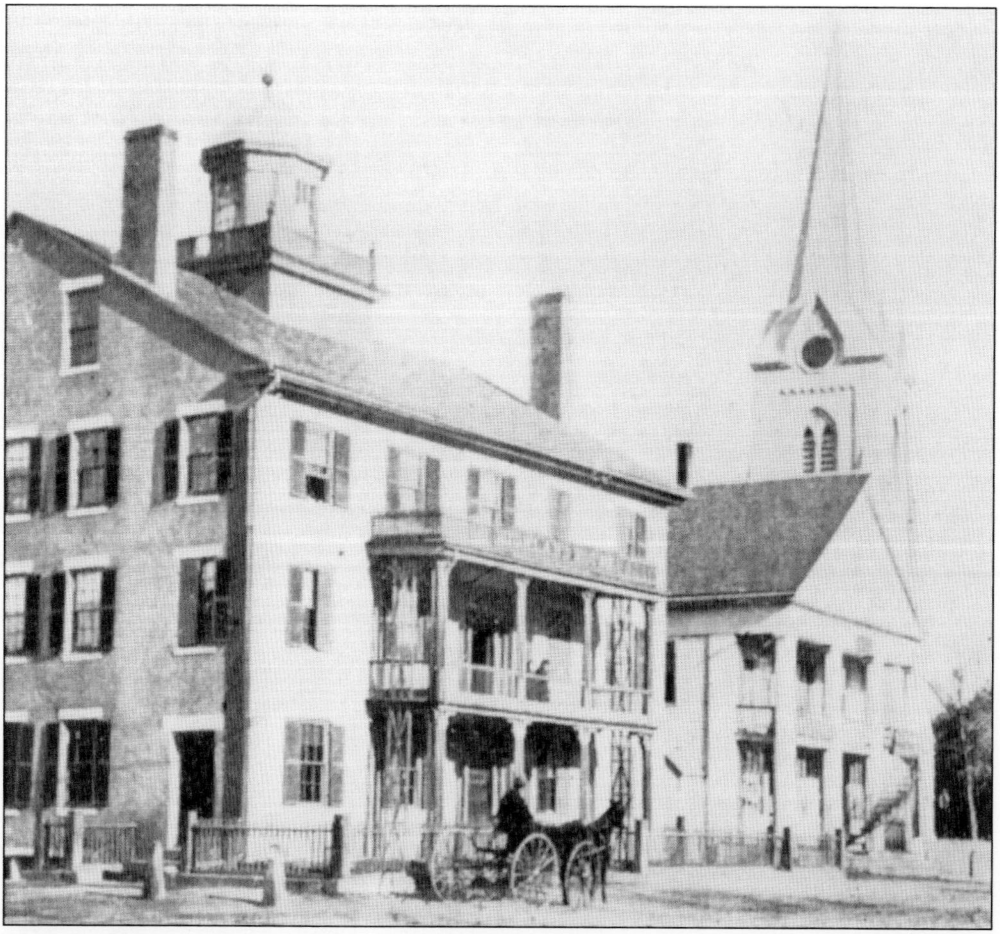

These buildings on Main Street near the First Congregational Church were photographed in the late 1800s.

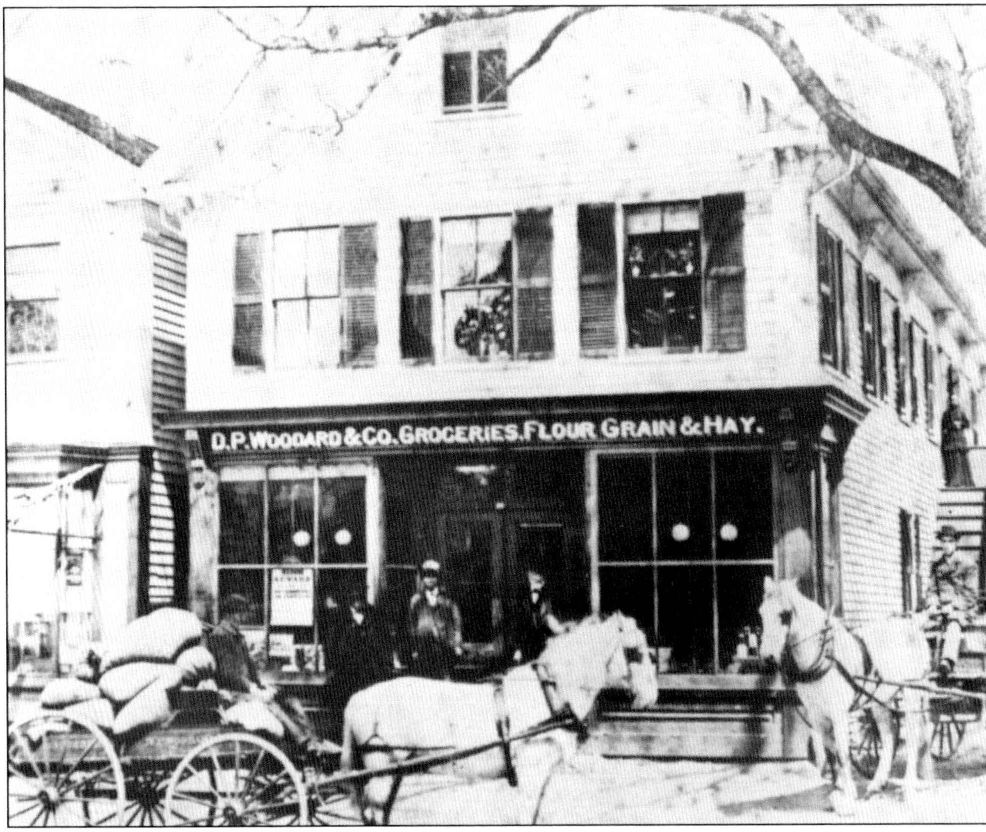

This old-time store was located on Main Street around 1900.

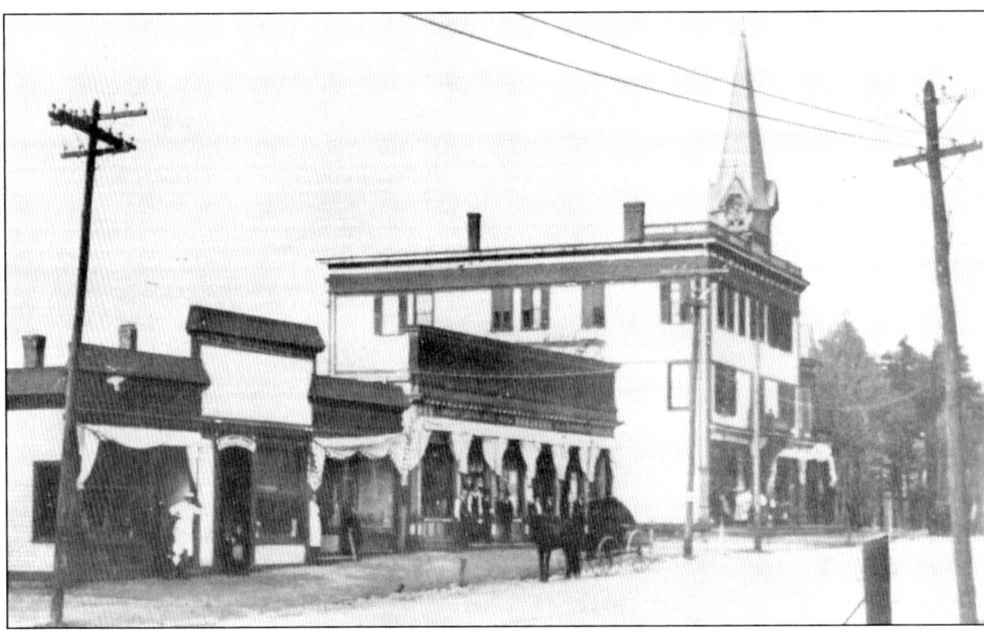
Main Street stores located near Hayden Rowe Street are shown here around 1900. The Congregational Church steeple can be seen on the far right.

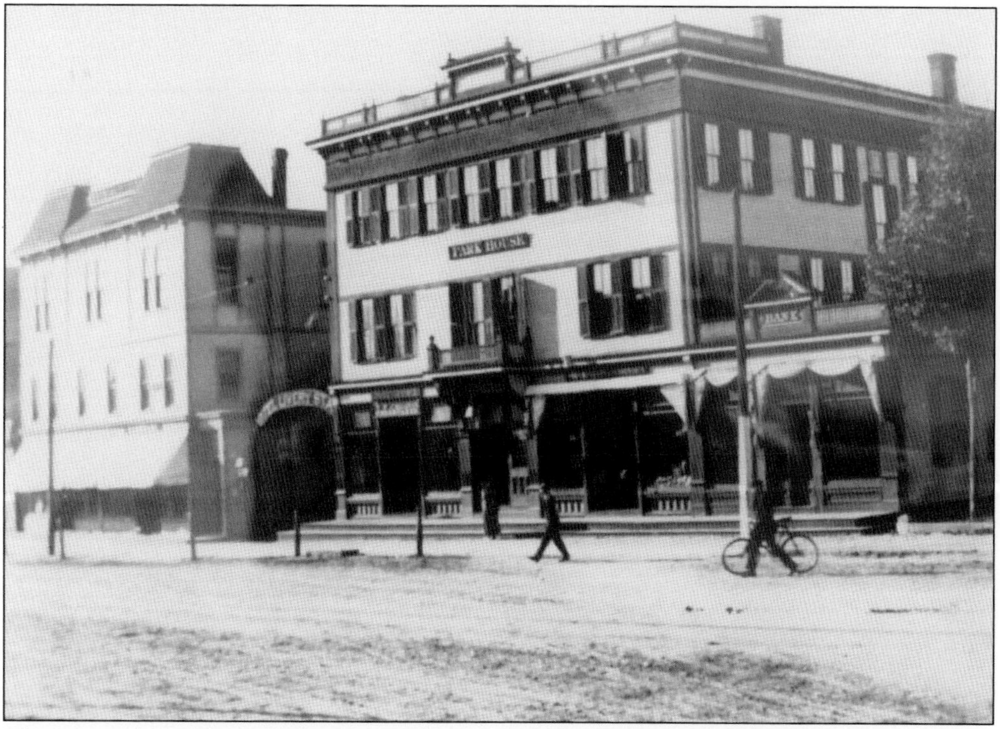

This image shows the Park House on Main Street around 1900. Callanan's wareroom, which was used for the display of caskets and coffins, was once located in this building.

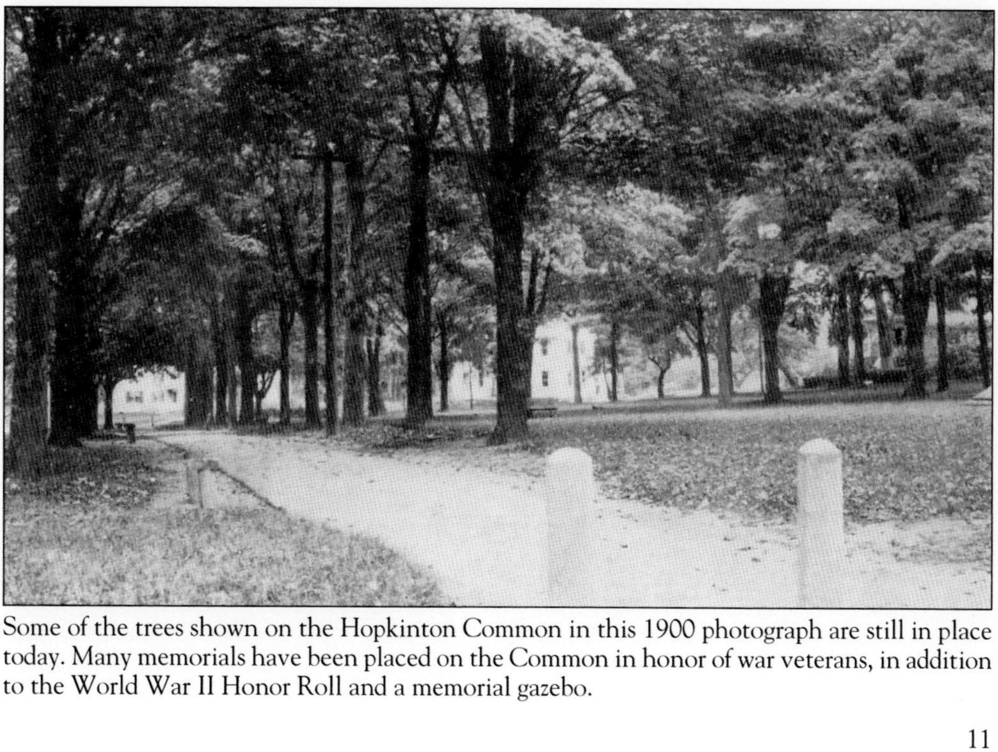

Some of the trees shown on the Hopkinton Common in this 1900 photograph are still in place today. Many memorials have been placed on the Common in honor of war veterans, in addition to the World War II Honor Roll and a memorial gazebo.

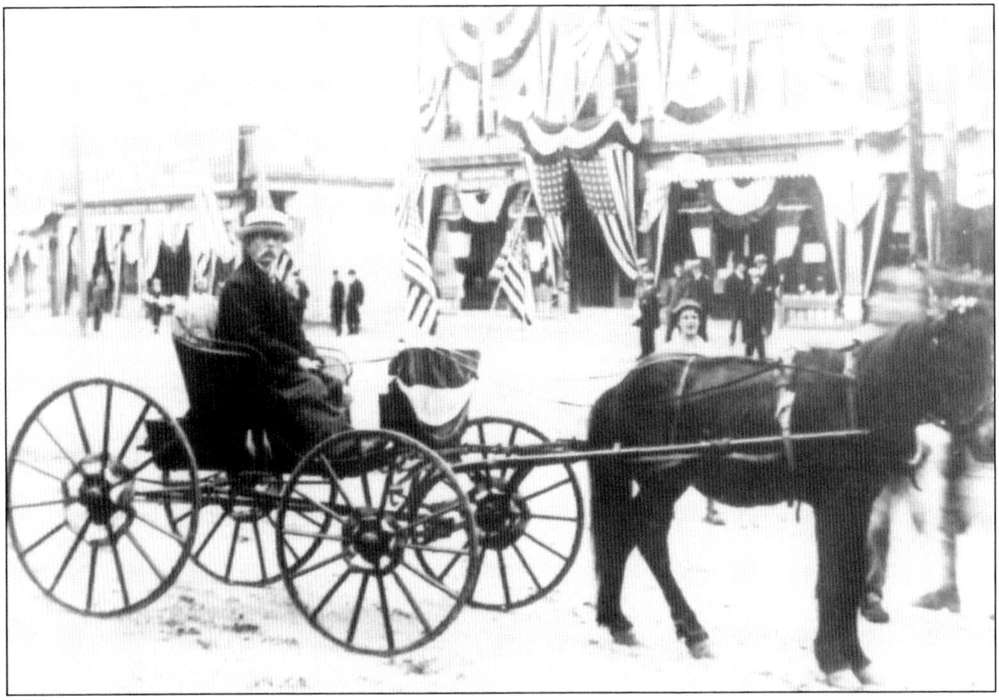

Michael Maloney was captured on film on Main Street during the 1915 town anniversary. The pony and wagon were owned by Phipps Moshier.

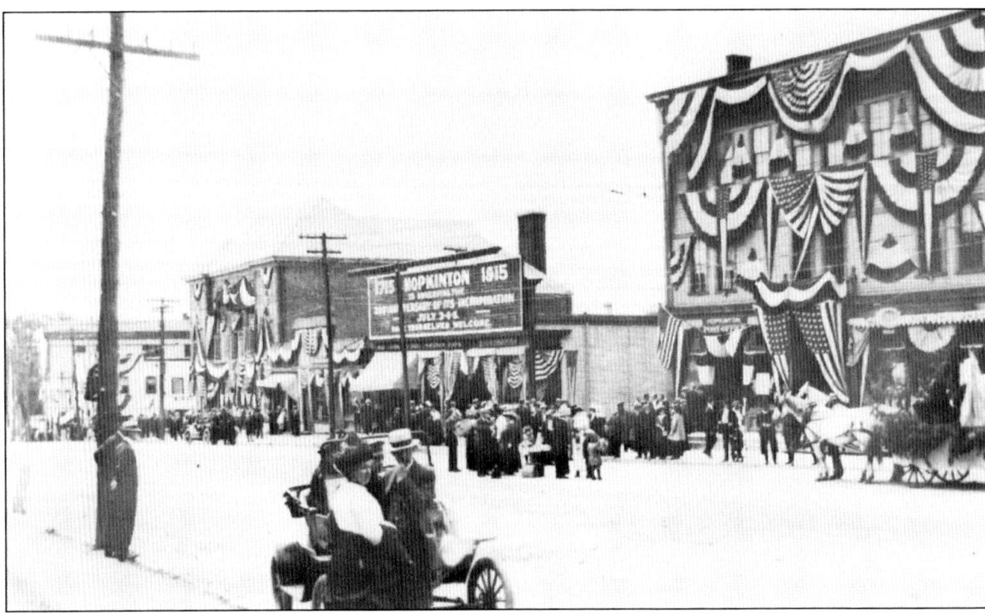

Bicentennial festivities were documented on the anniversary of the town's 1715 incorporation. This view is looking west on Main Street. Note the post office near the center of the picture. The town hall is seen near the left-hand side of the photograph.

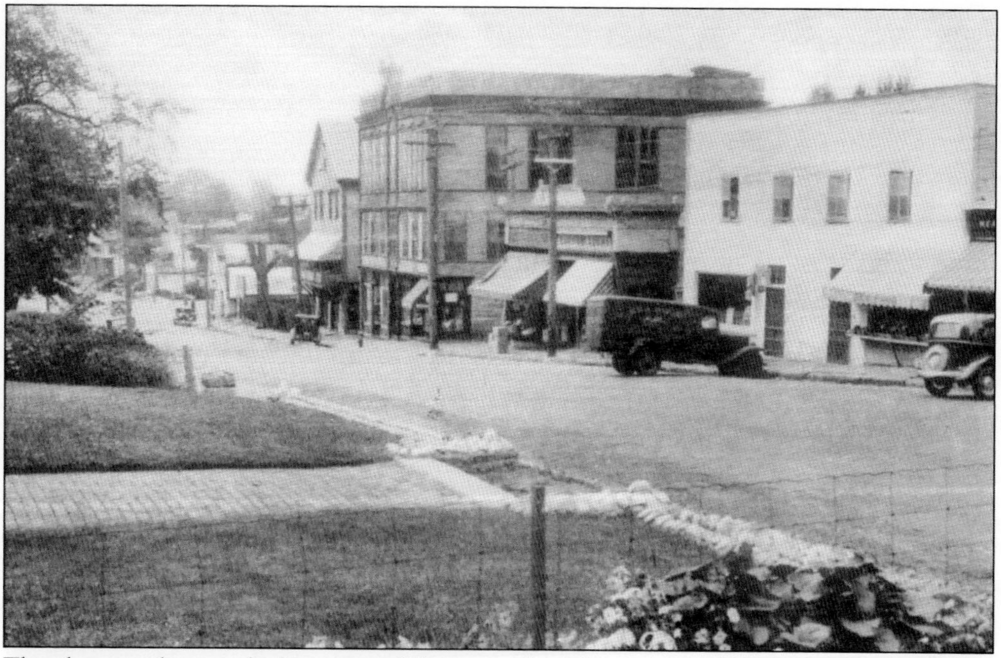

The photographer was looking toward the west when this picture of Main Street was taken in the late 1930s.

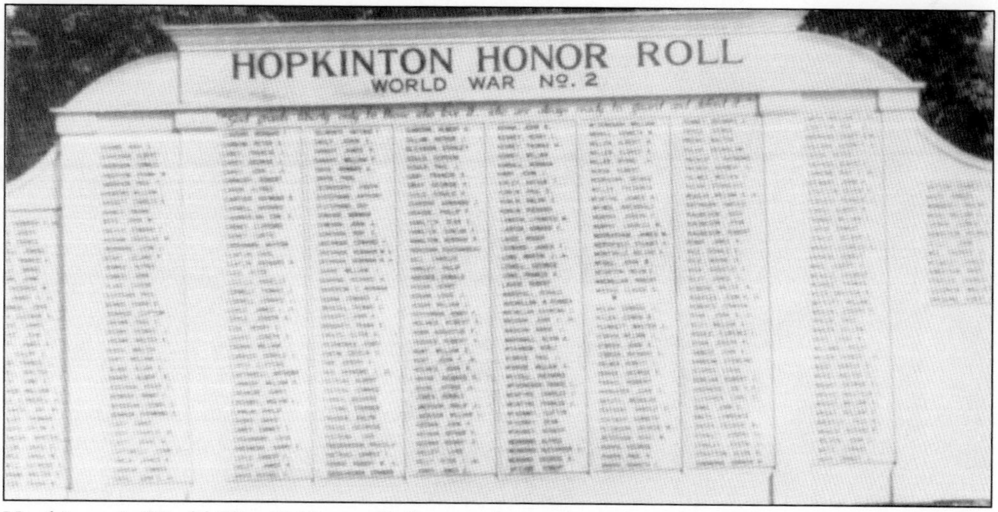

Hopkinton's World War II Honor Roll, once located on the edge of the town common, was dedicated on May 2, 1943.

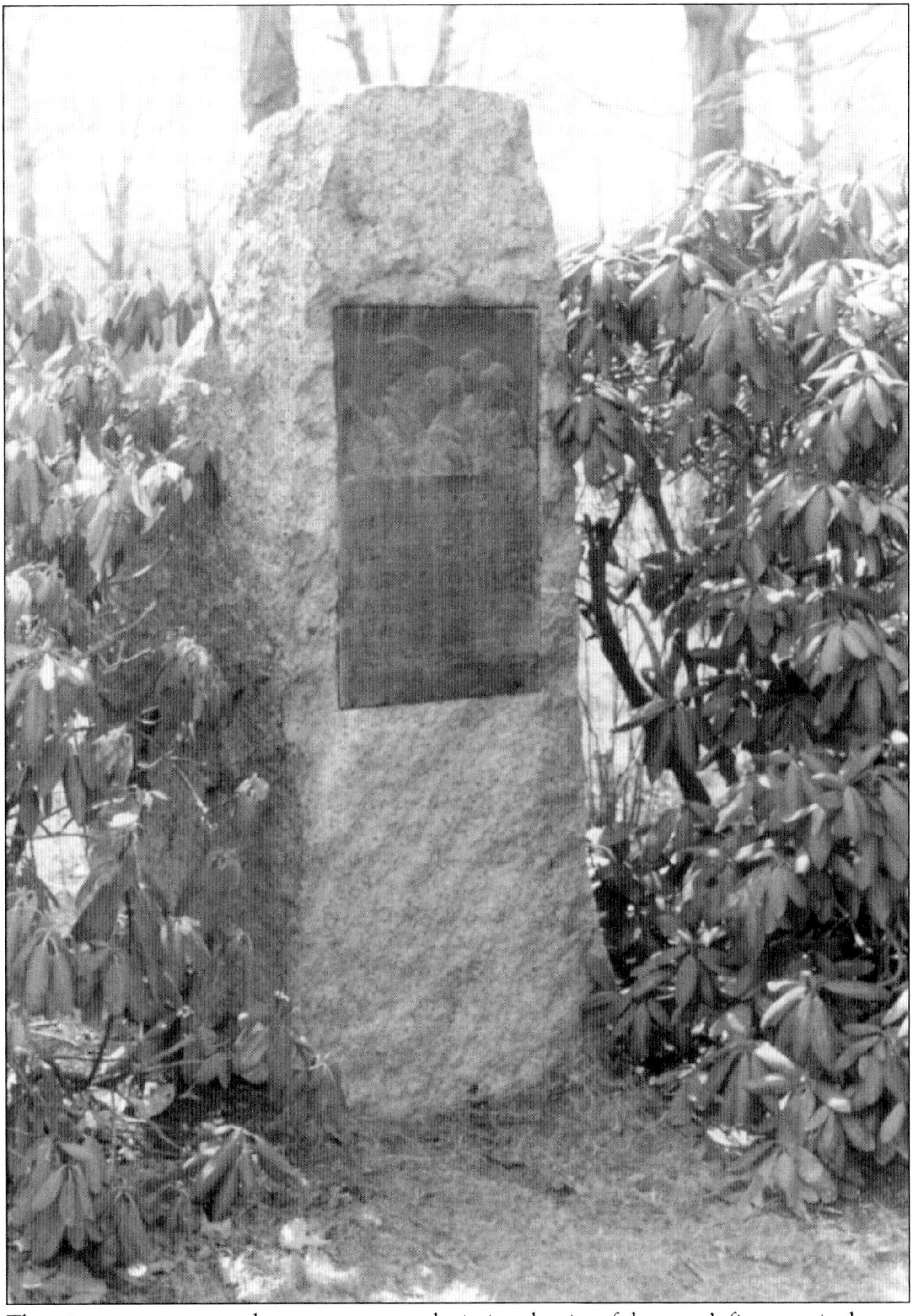

There is a monument on the town common depicting the site of the town's first meetinghouse.

Two

Businesses

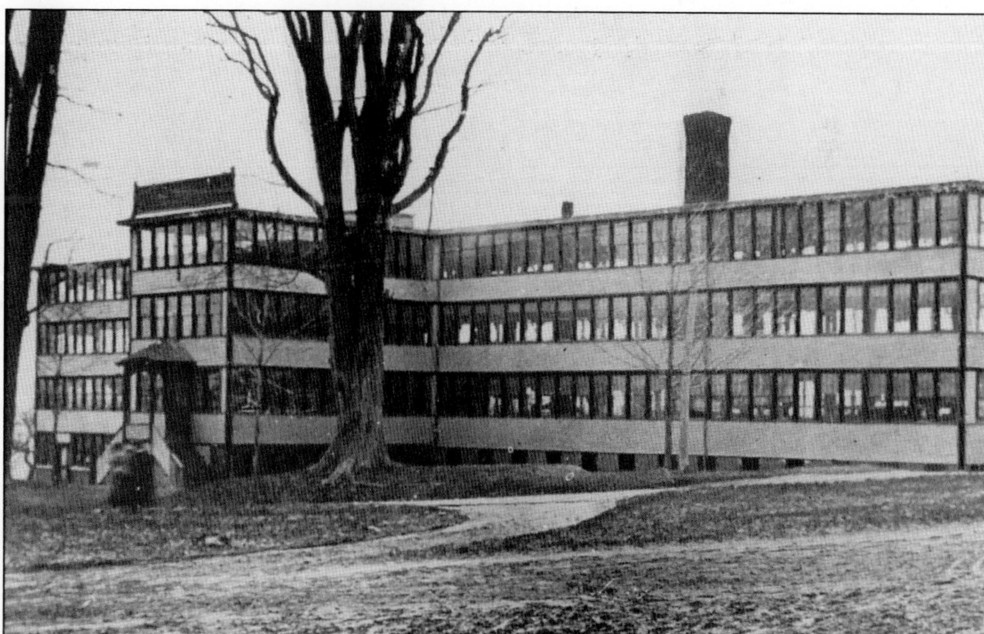

The Imperial shoe factory was one of the many boot and shoe industries that flourished at one time in Hopkinton.

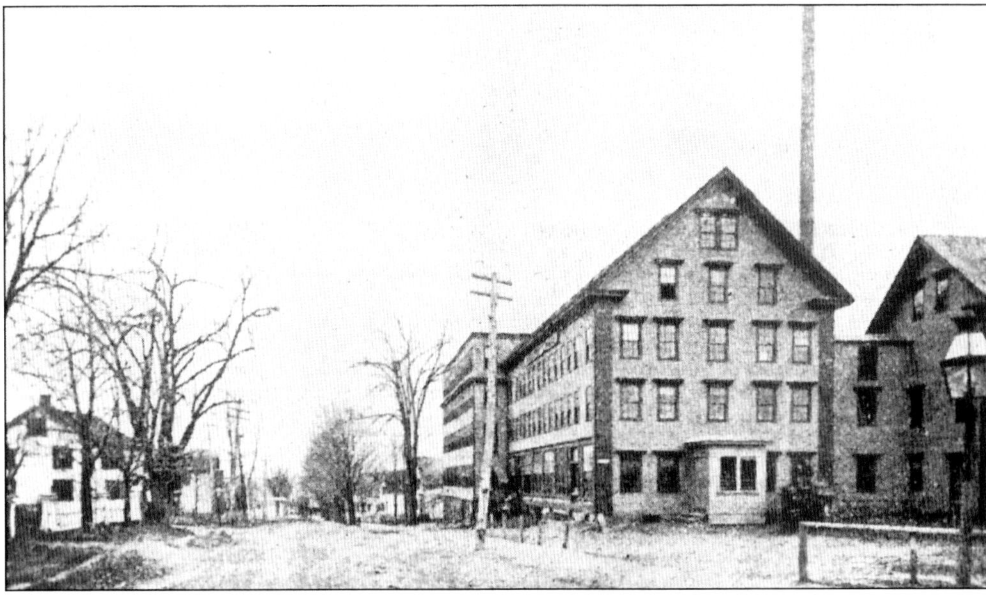

The Davenport block on Main Street was once occupied by a boot and shoe shop.

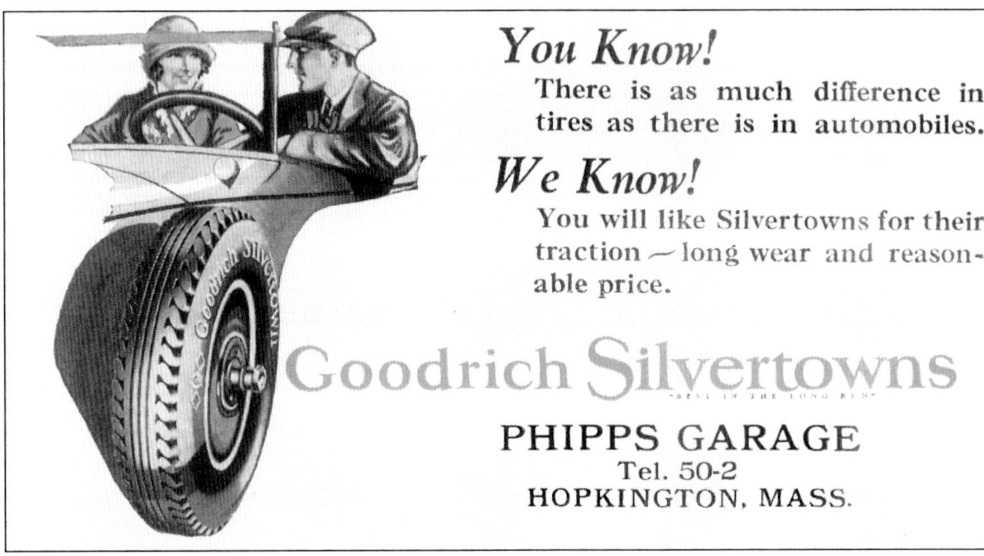

A 1930 automobile tire advertisement promotes Phipps Garage, then located on Main Street. Note that Hopkinton was misspelled on this desk blotter by the advertiser.

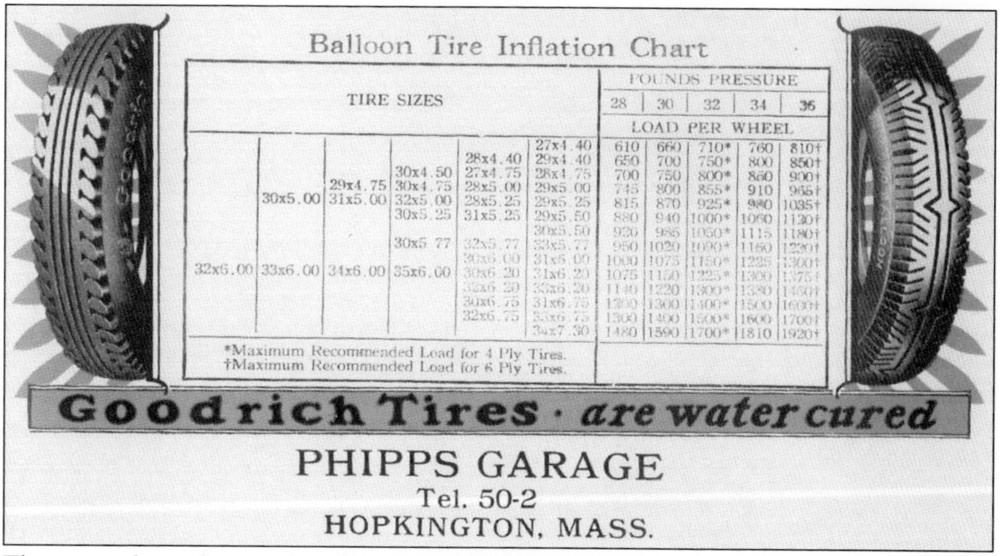

This image shows that another sharp advertisement was designed for Phipps Garage in 1930.

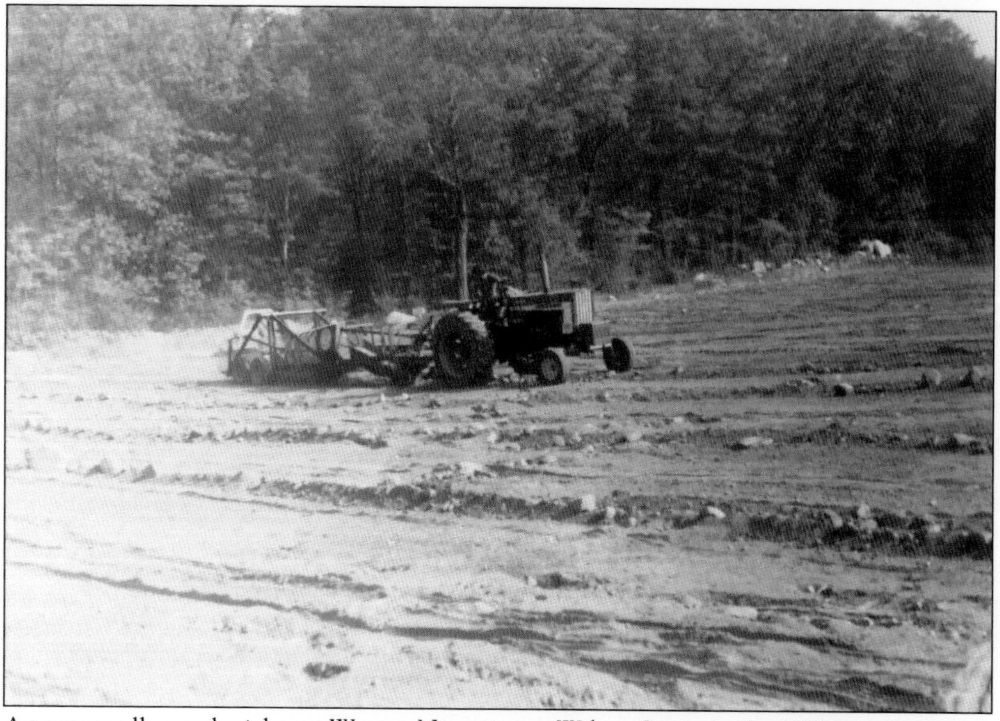

A tractor pulls a rock picker at Weston Nurseries on Wilson Street in the 1980s.

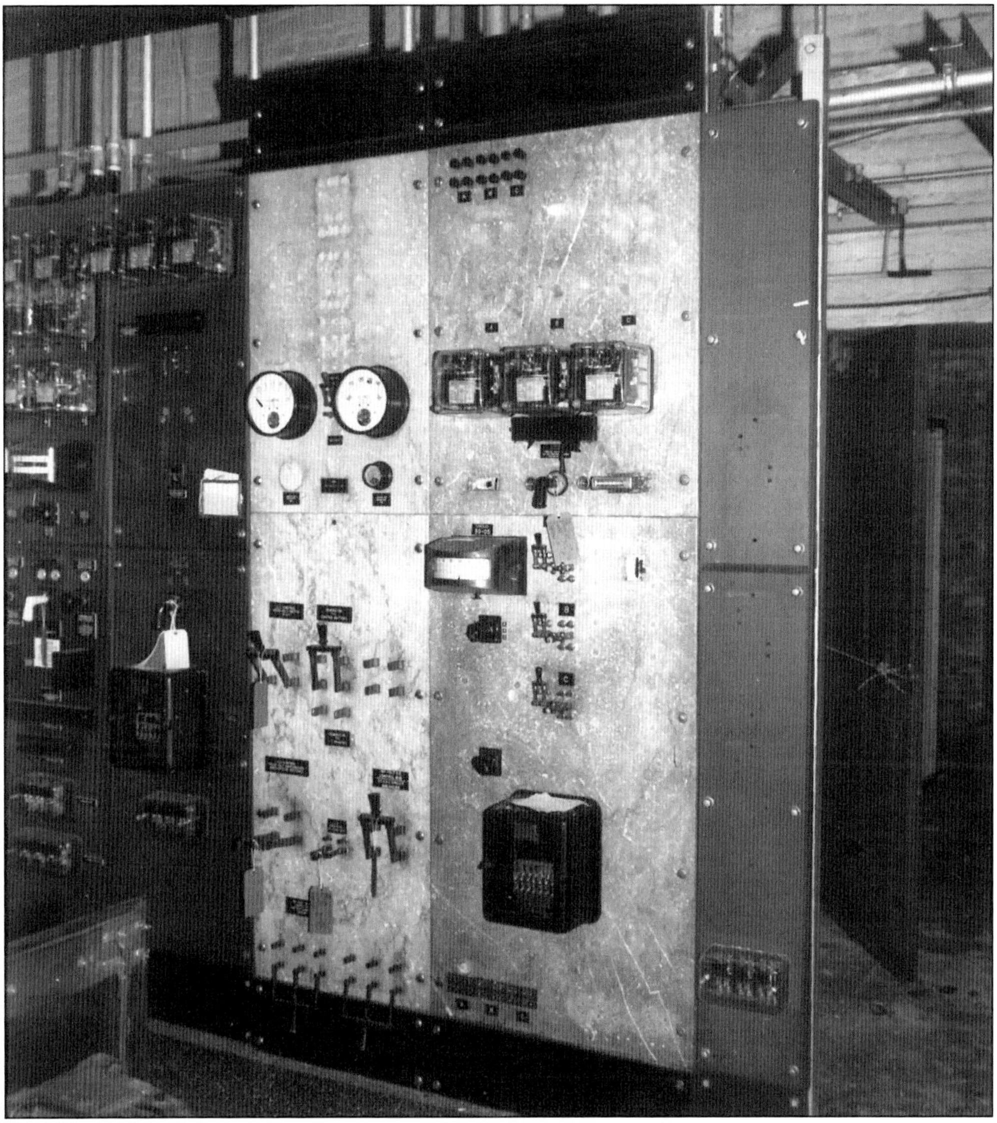

Here is one of the control panels located inside the Boston Edison Station #35 on East Main Street in the 1980s.

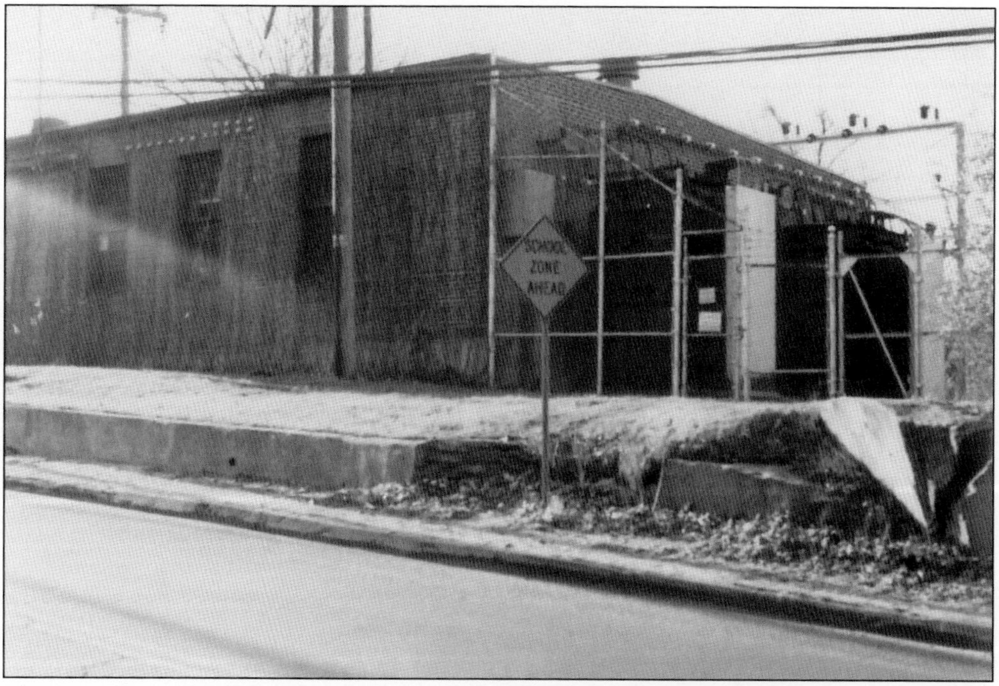

This view shows the former Boston Edison switching station on East Main Street.

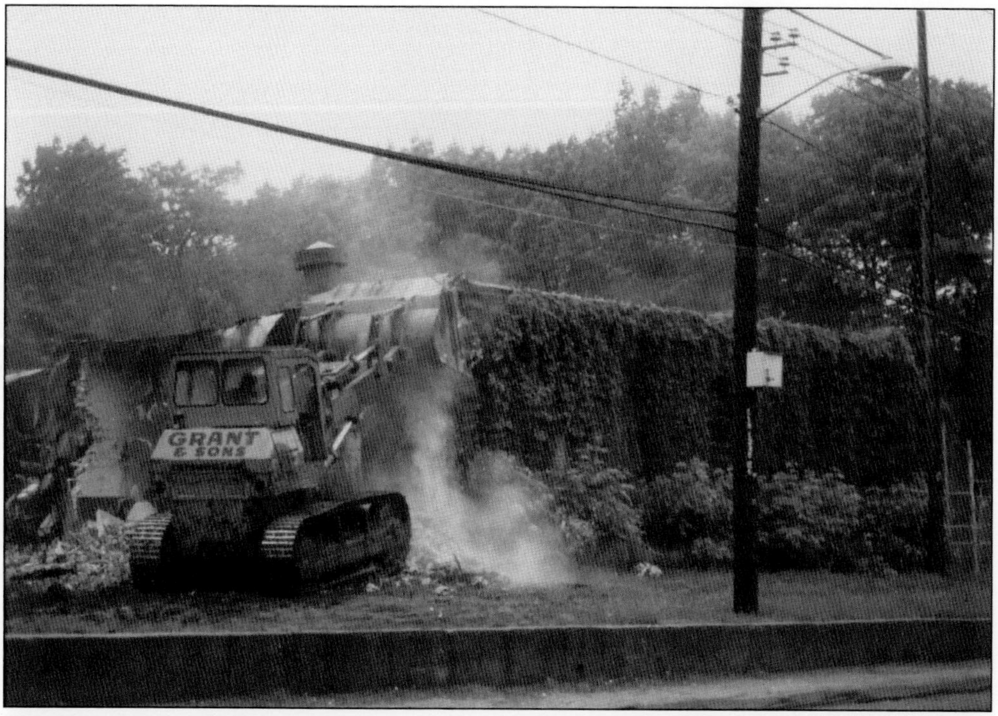

The demolition of the Edison station took place on June 3, 1981. The building had been erected in 1907.

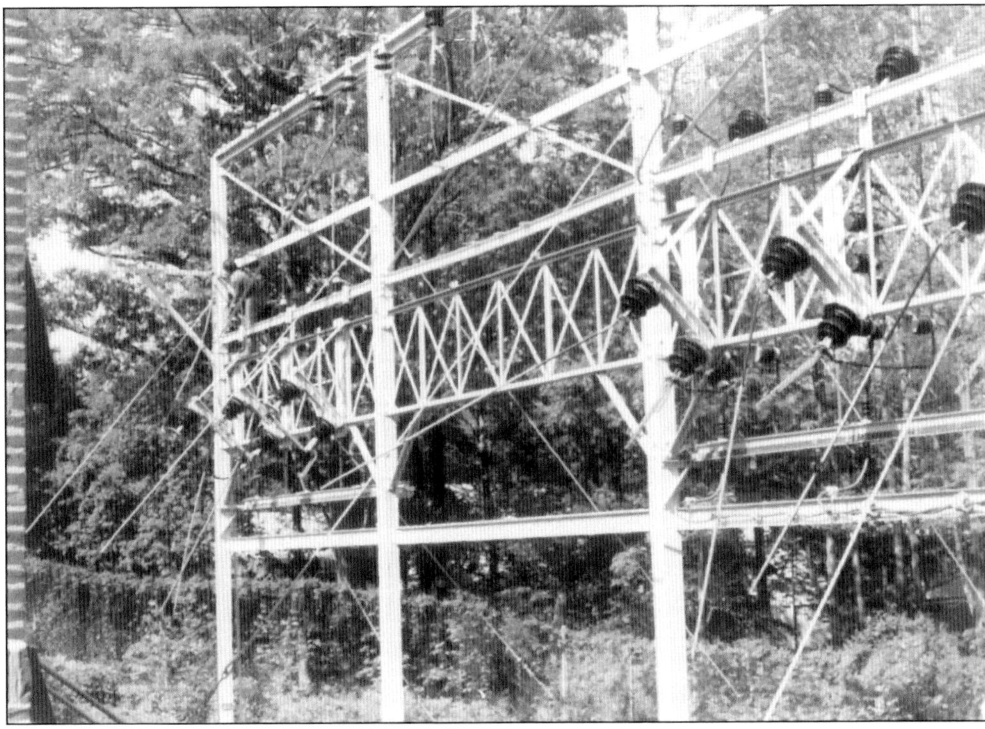

This steel terminal framework was part of the Edison installation.

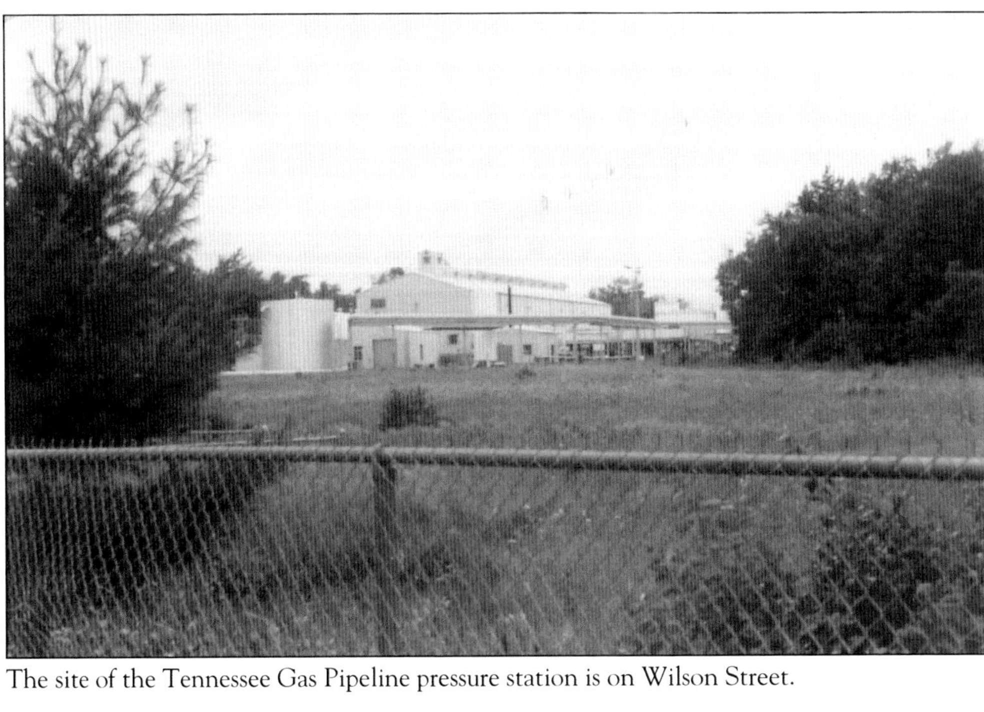

The site of the Tennessee Gas Pipeline pressure station is on Wilson Street.

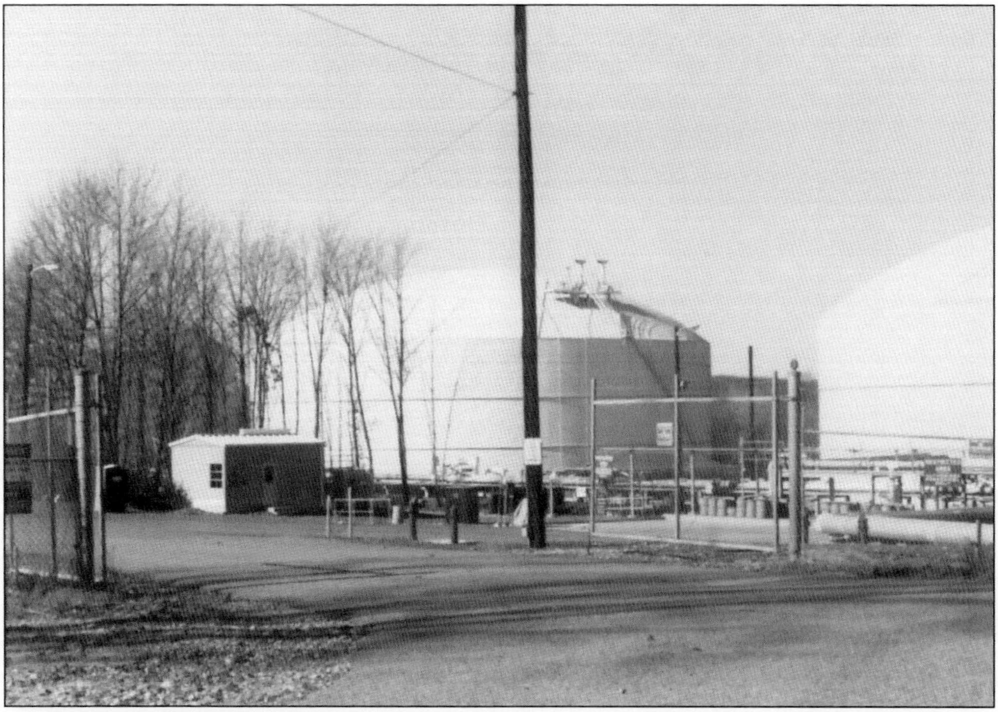

Tennessee Gas Pipeline storage tanks are located at the intersection of Wilson Street and Rafferty Road.

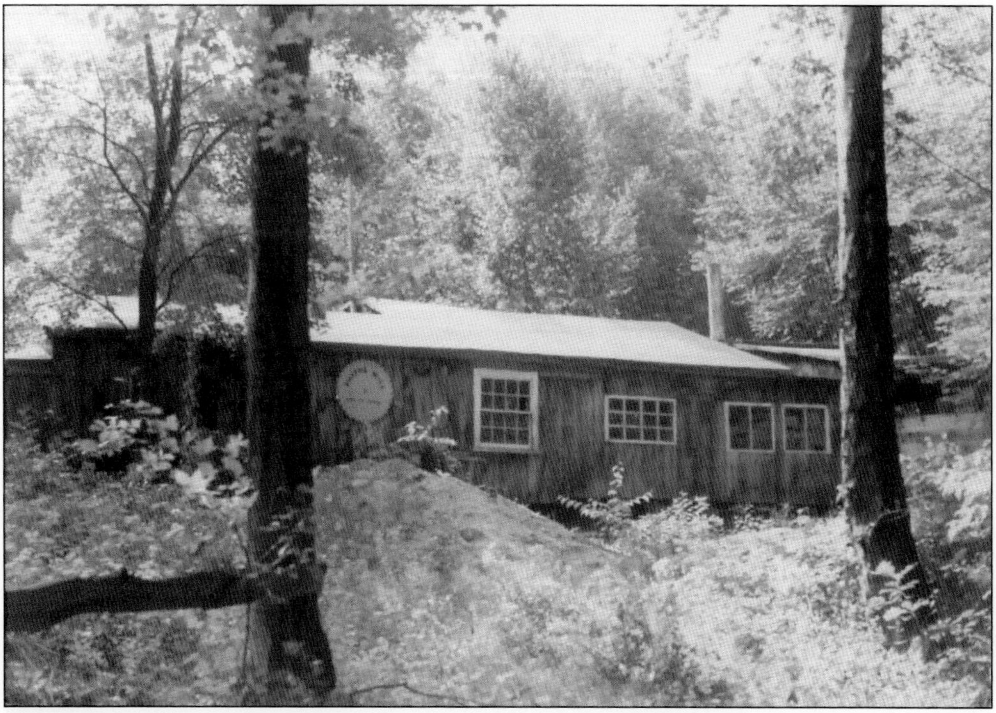

Phipps's sawmill on Winter Street is one of the three sawmills located in Hopkinton.

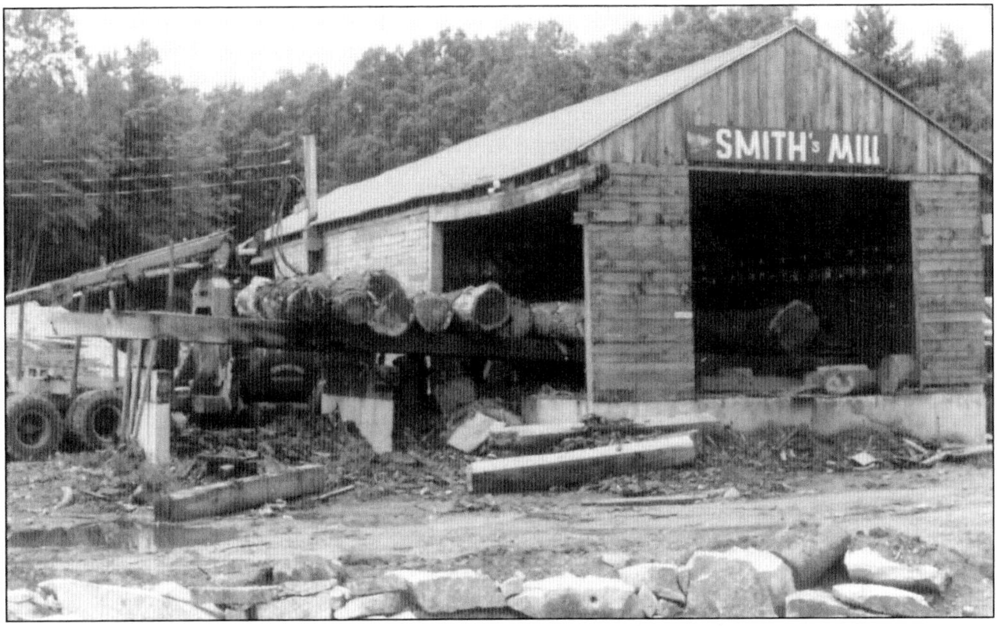

Smith's sawmill is another privately owned operation located on Wilson Street.

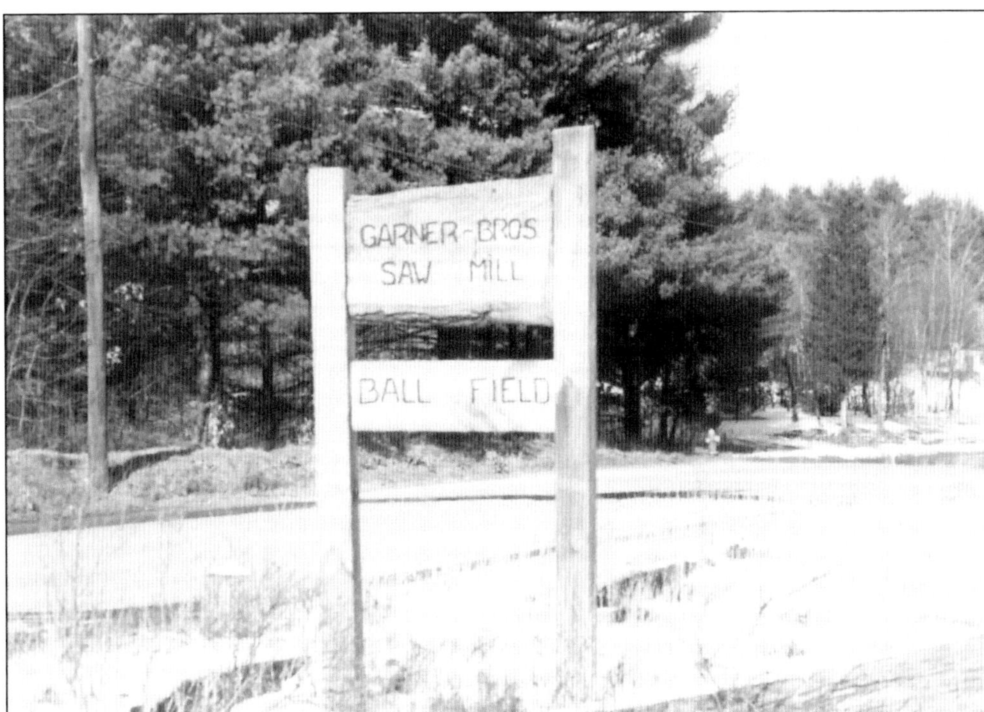

This sign identifies the Garner Bros. sawmill located off Fruit Street.

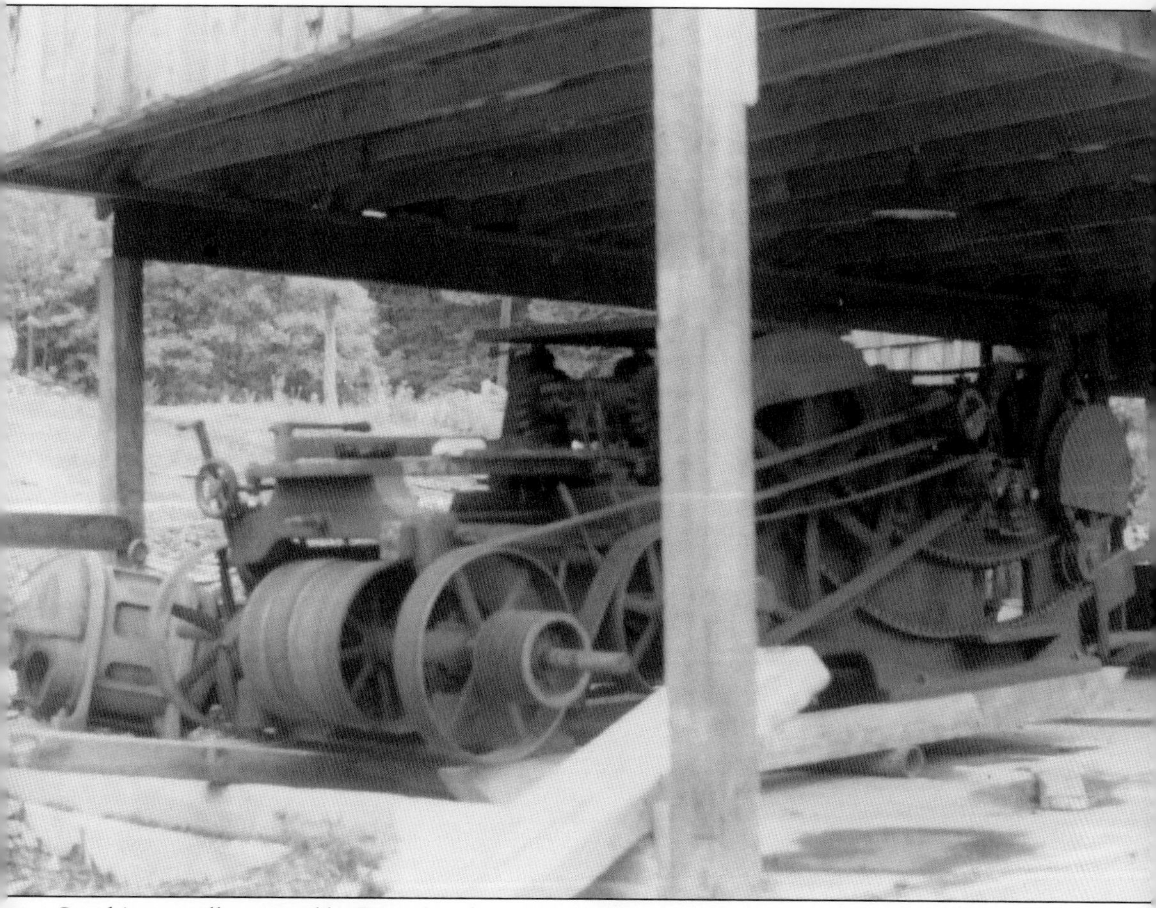

Smith's sawmill is owned by Barry Smith and it is still in operation.

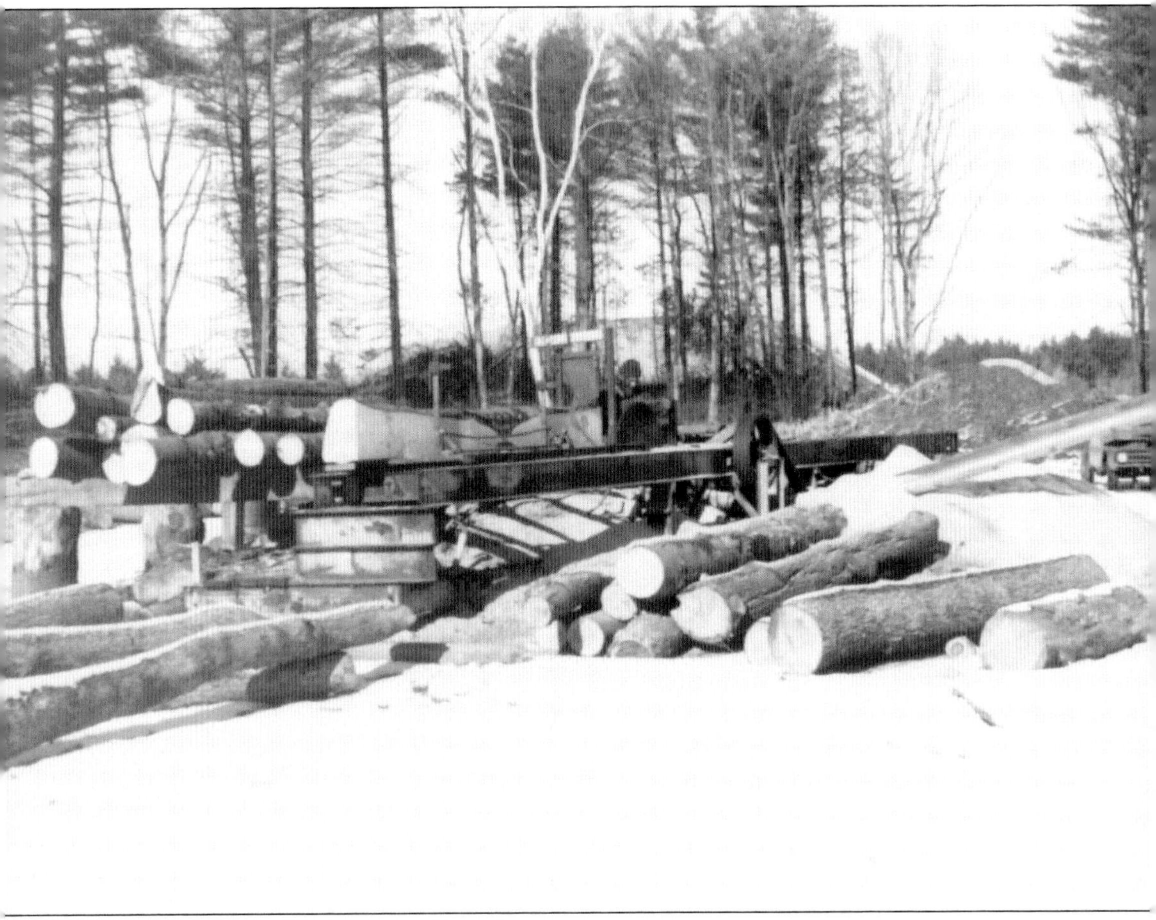

A portion of the Garner sawmill indicates an ongoing operation.

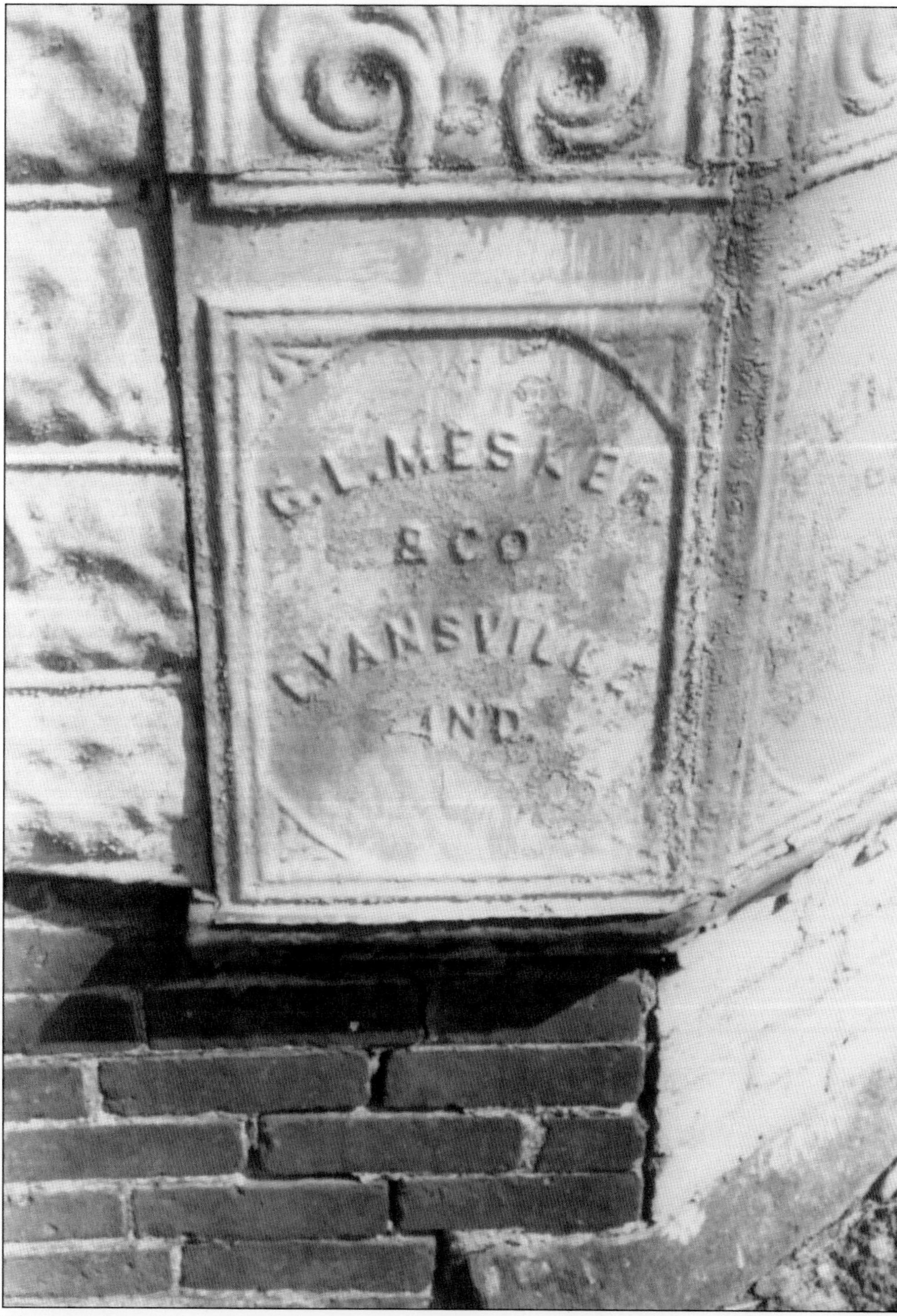

The manufacturer's name can be seen on the material used to cover the outside of this motor parts building on Main Street after its renovation.

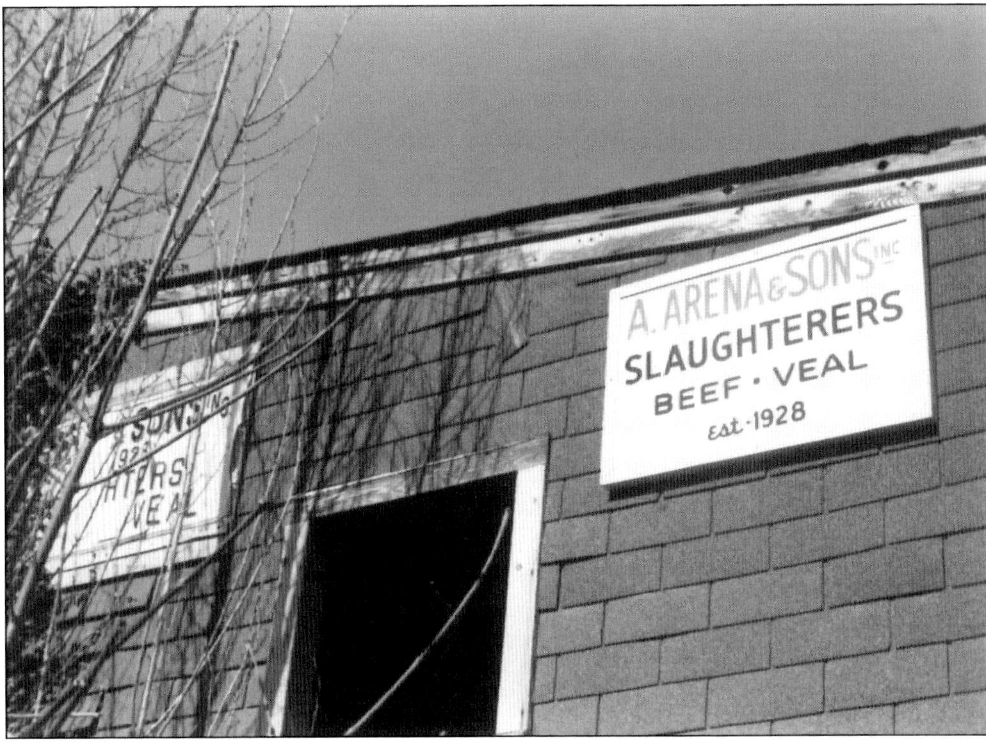

This sign identifies the Arena slaughterhouse at 159 Ash Street.

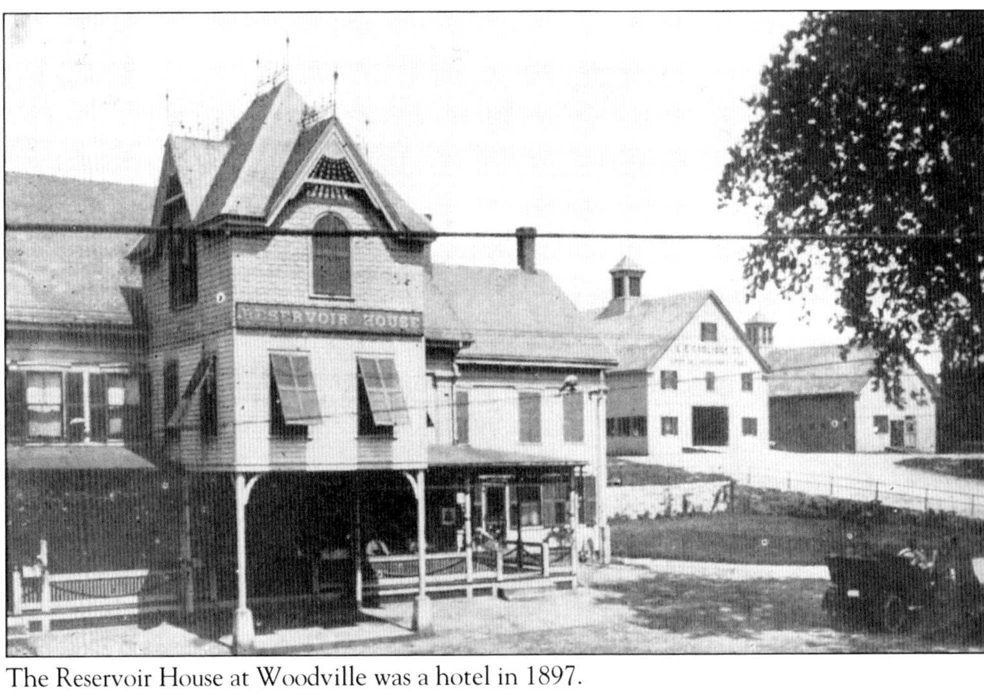

The Reservoir House at Woodville was a hotel in 1897.

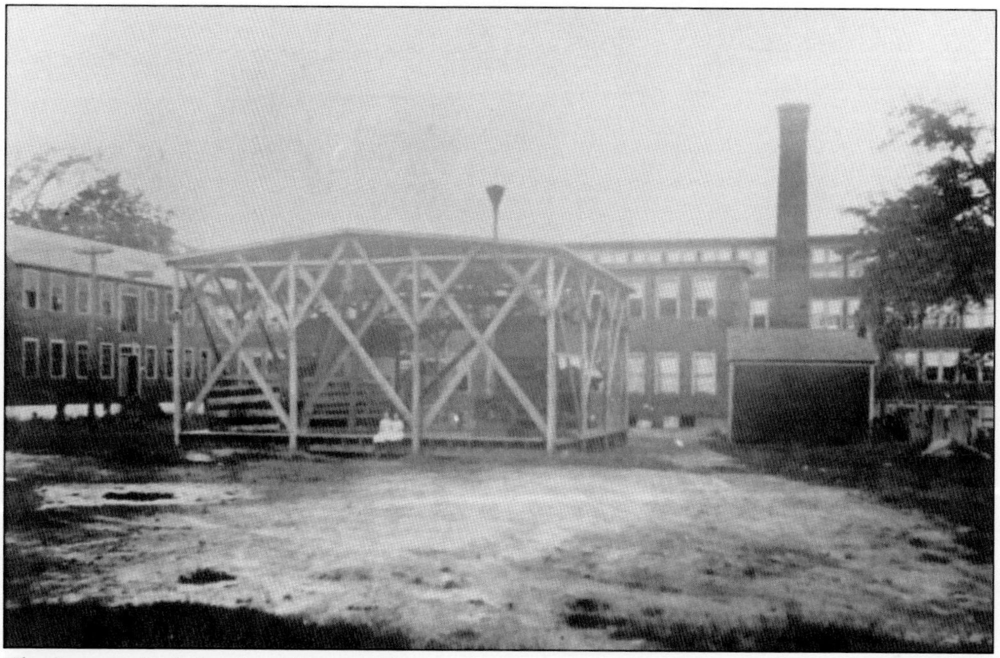

The Lawson Pink Food and Proctor Co. was located on Hayden Rowe Street.

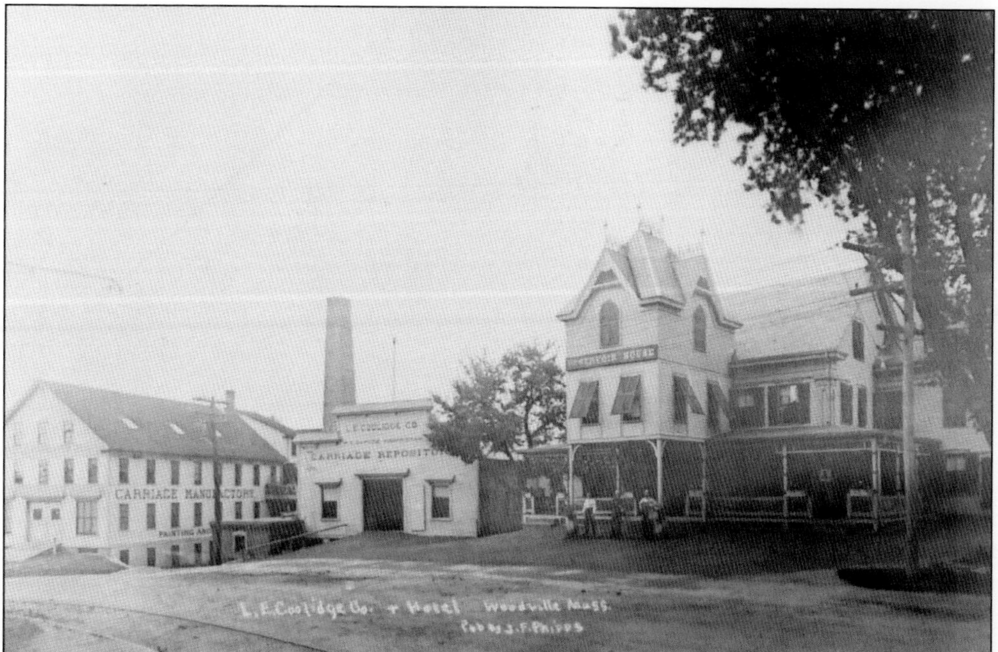

The Coolidge carriage factory, a repository, and the Reservoir House (seen from left to right) at Woodville were owned by L.E. Coolidge.

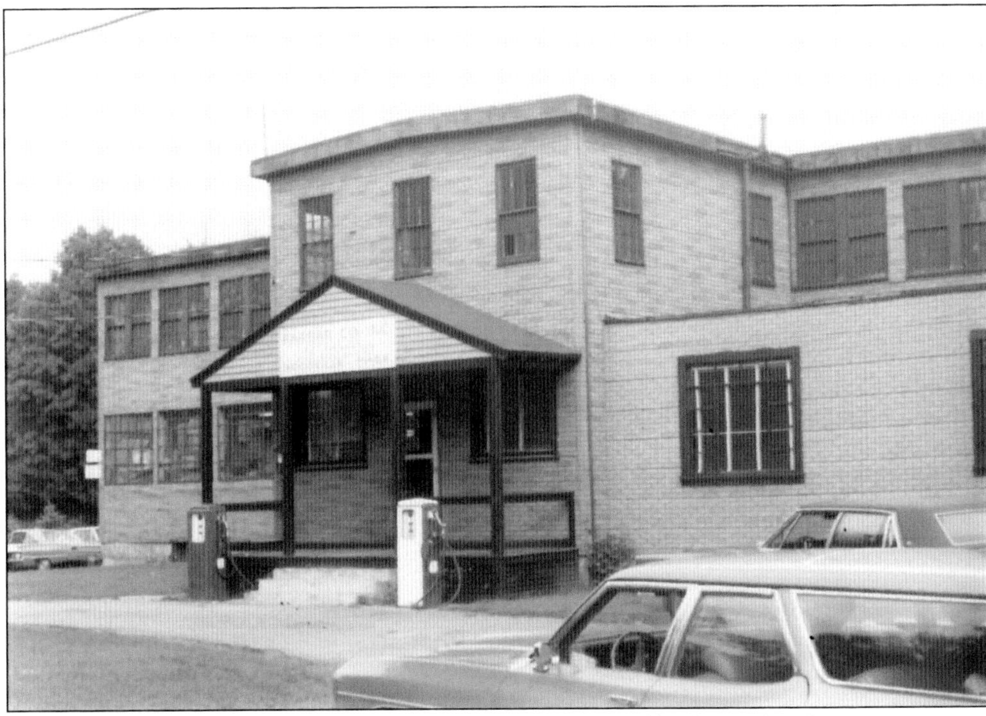

A firetruck factory on Winter Street in Woodville was owned by Farrar Co., Inc.

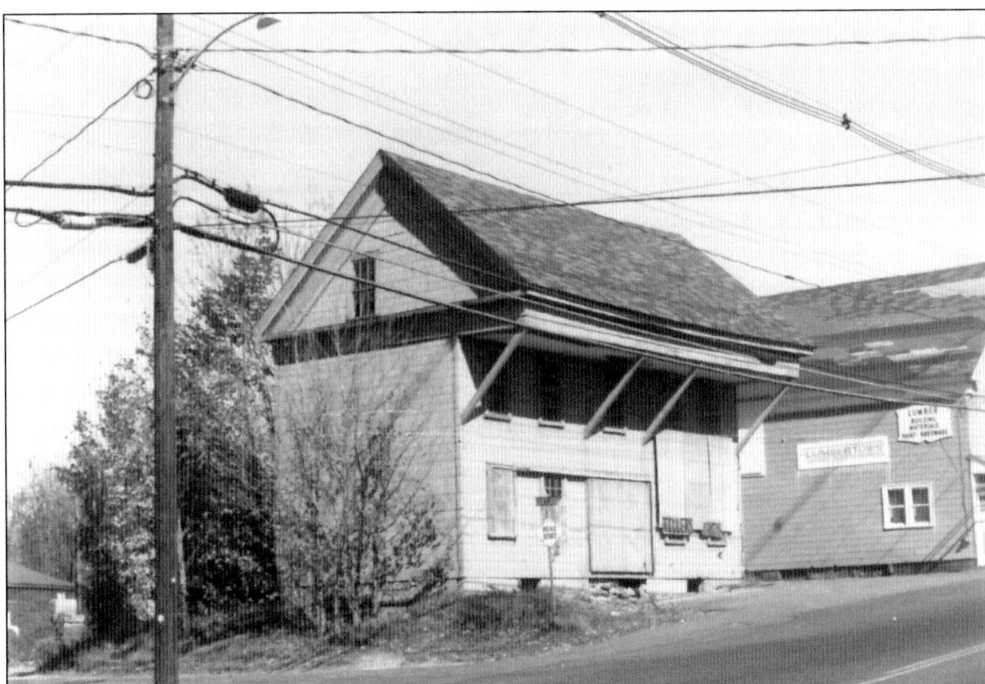

This building on Main Street was used for many years by Lumbertown.

Three

Schools and Town Hall

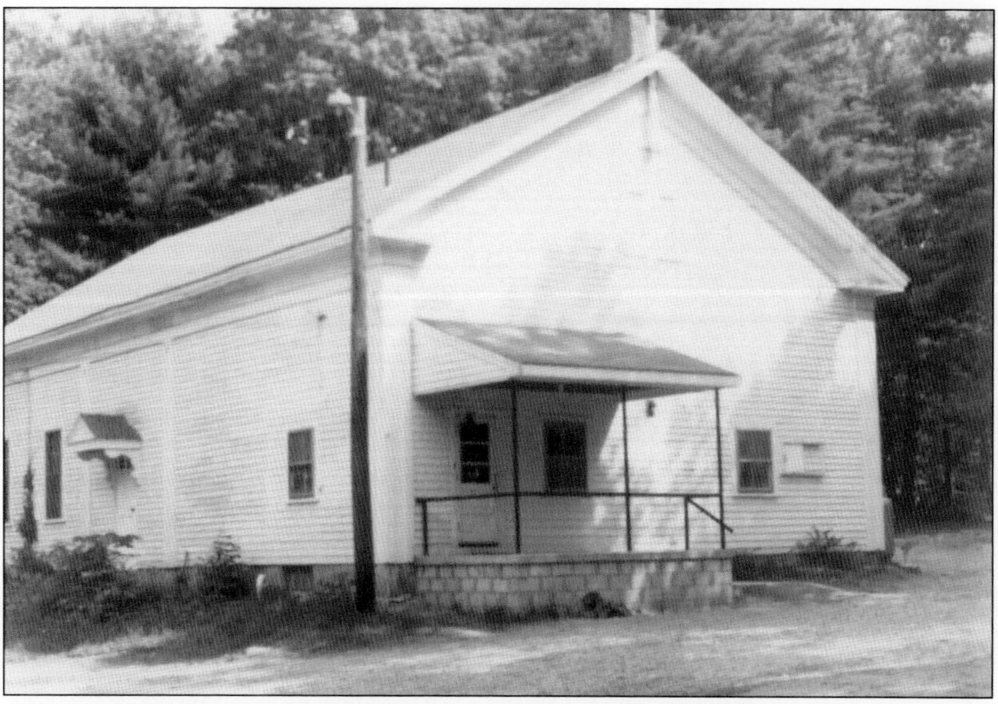

This elementary school at Woodville is now owned by the Woodville Rod and Gun Club.

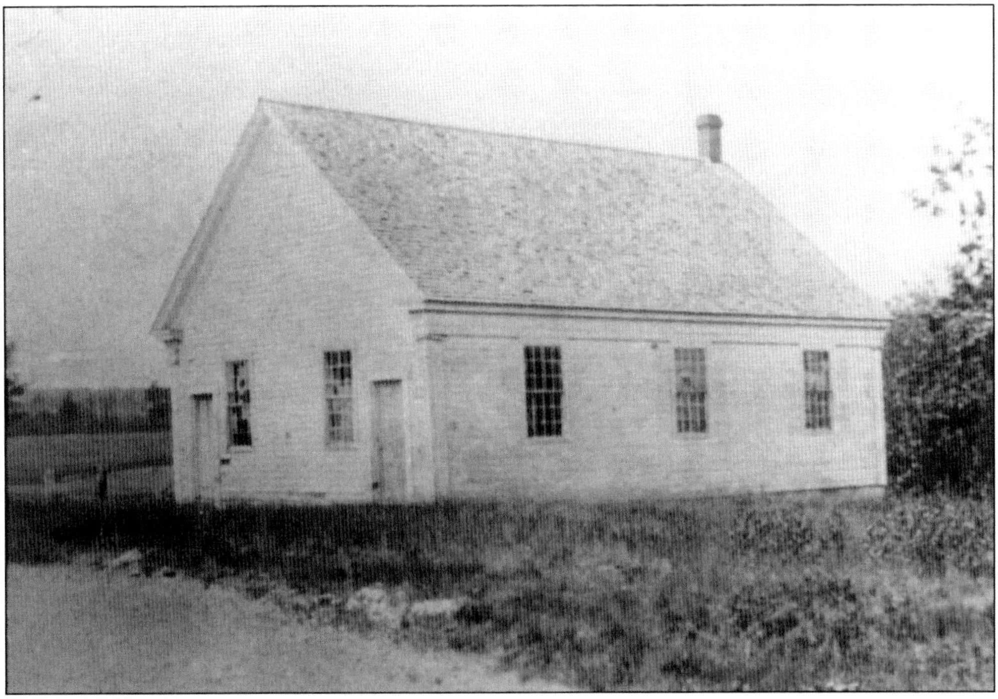

The Number 6 schoolhouse was at the intersection of Fruit and North Streets in 1900.

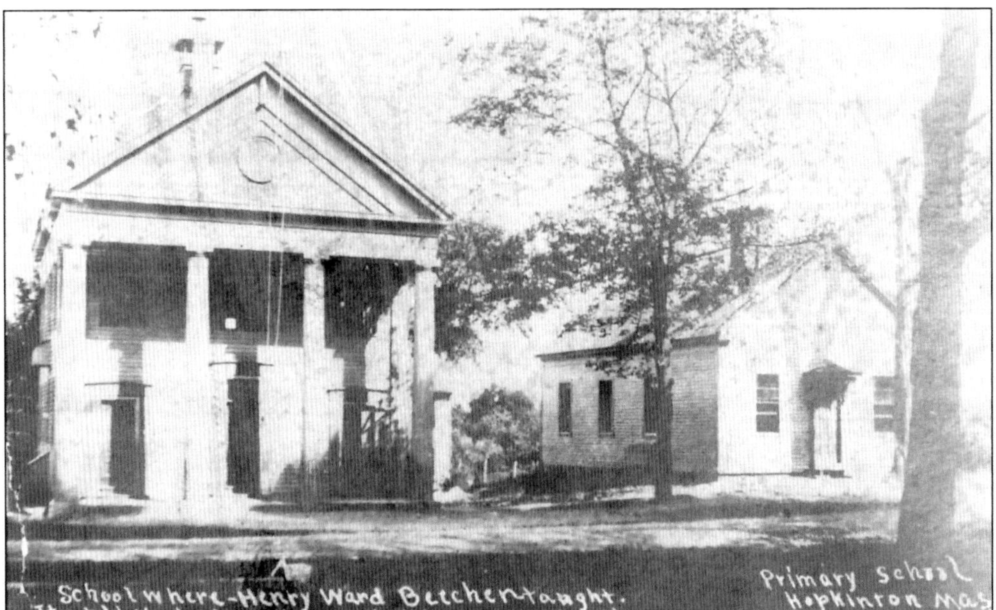

These were old school buildings on Ash Street. Henry Ward Beecher reportedly was once a teacher in the building on the left.

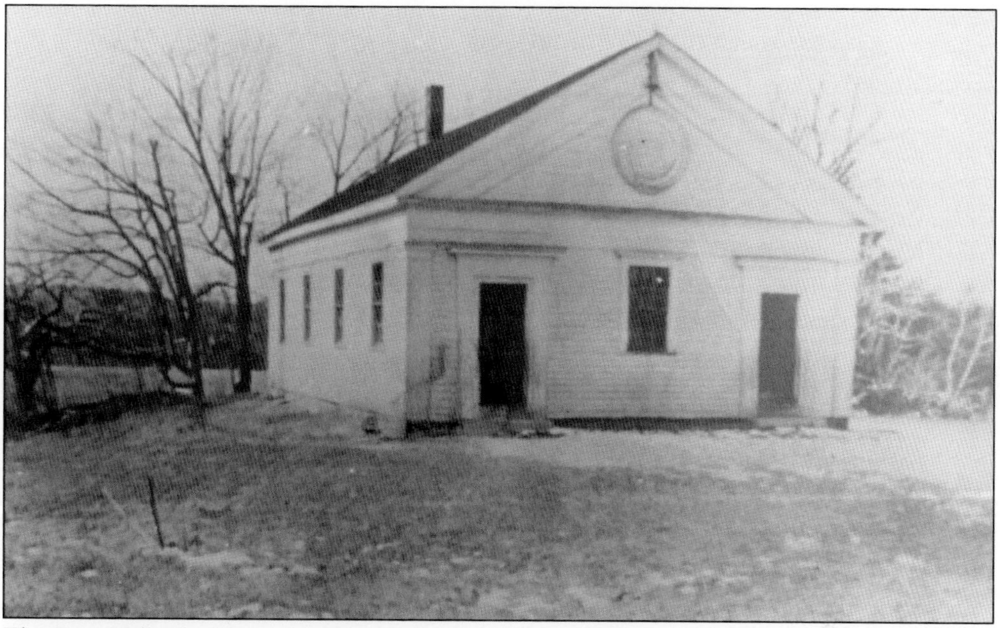

The Bear Hill schoolhouse, located on School Street, became a community building after it burned in 1950.

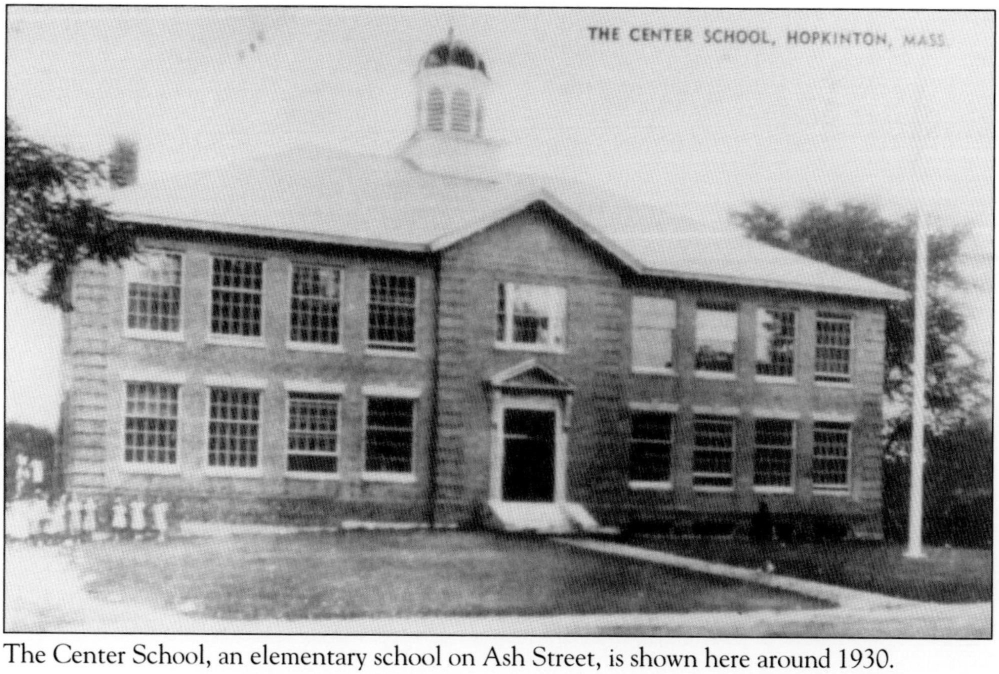

The Center School, an elementary school on Ash Street, is shown here around 1930.

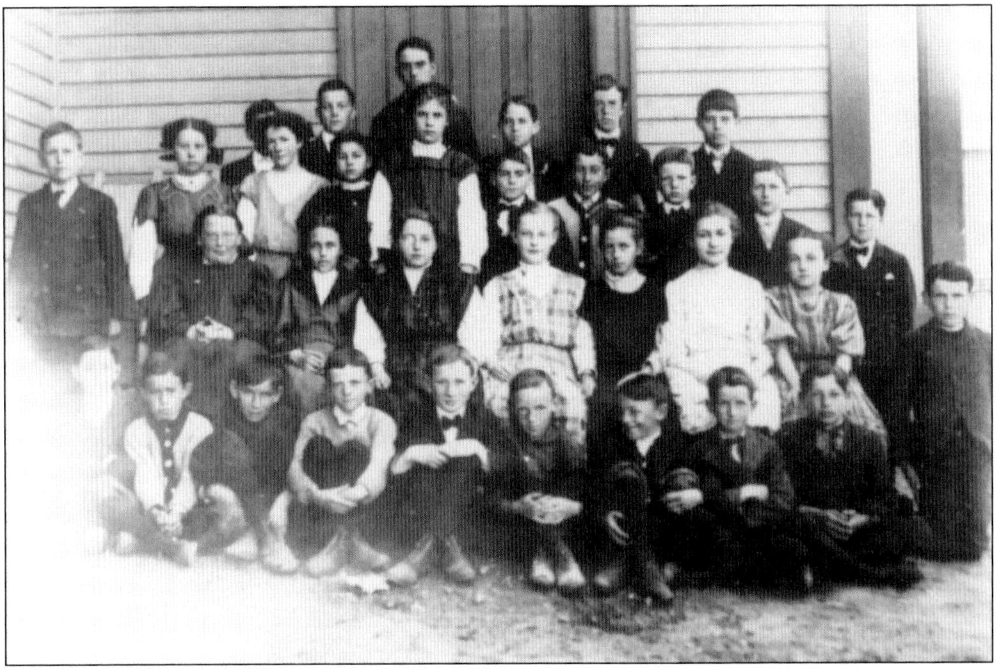

This is a sixth-grade class picture that was taken in 1909.

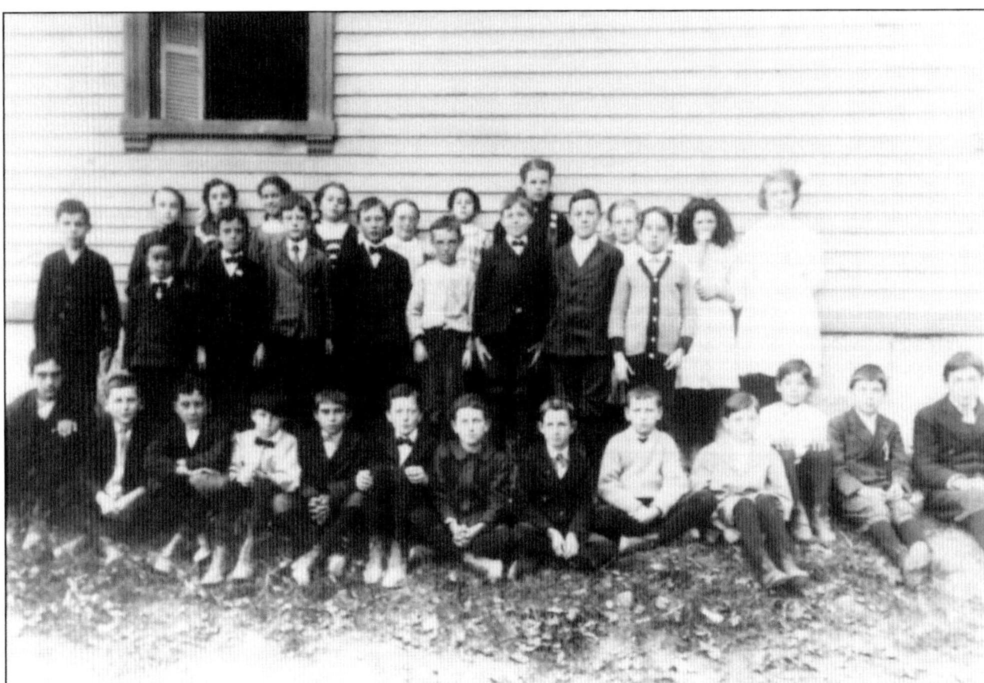

This is another 1909 school picture.

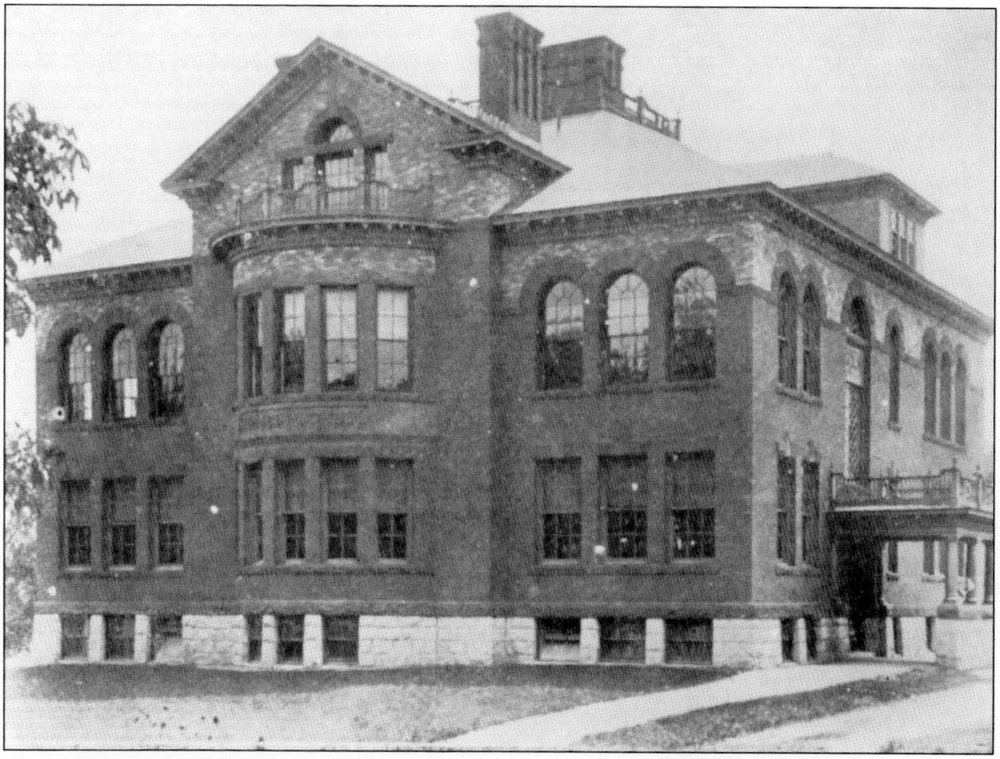

The old high school building on Main Street is now used by several businesses.

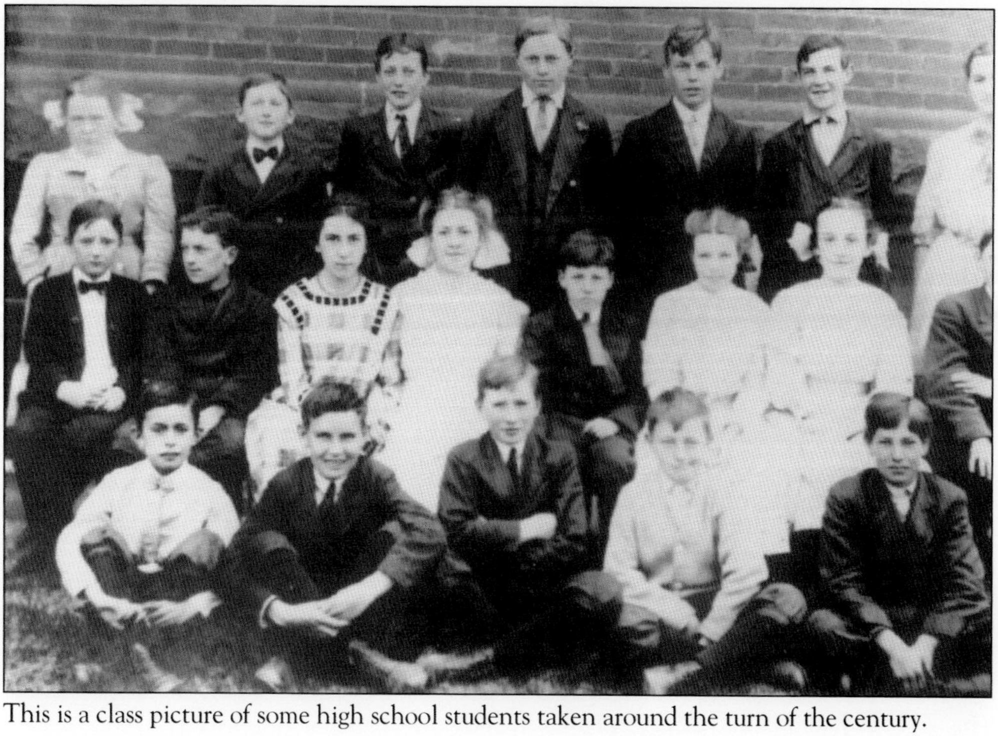

This is a class picture of some high school students taken around the turn of the century.

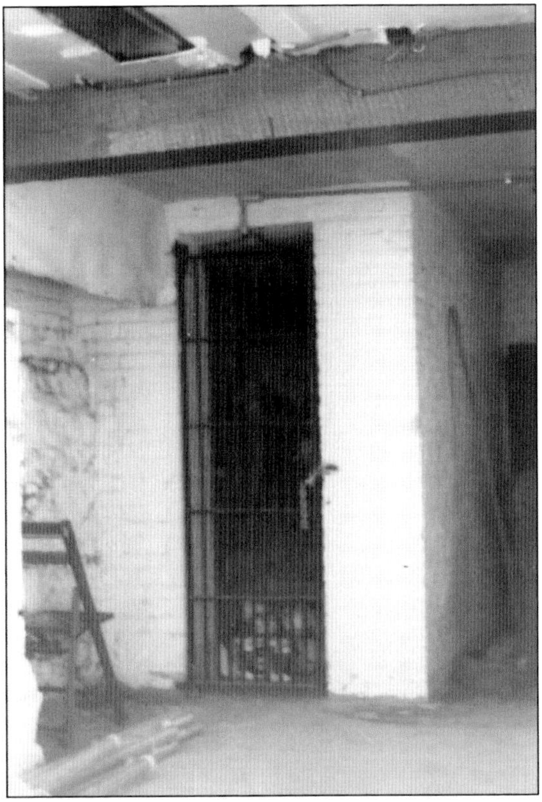

Three jail cells were once located in the basement of the town hall. Here we can see one of them. They were eliminated when the building was renovated in the late 1980s.

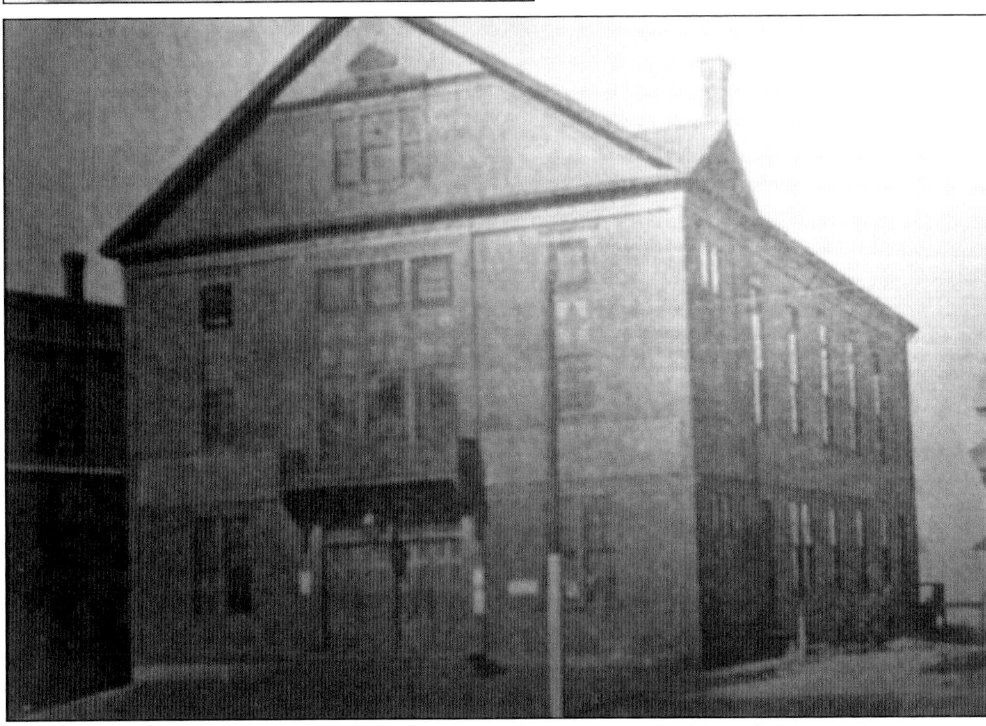

The old town hall on Main Street was built in 1883 and destroyed by a fire in 1900.

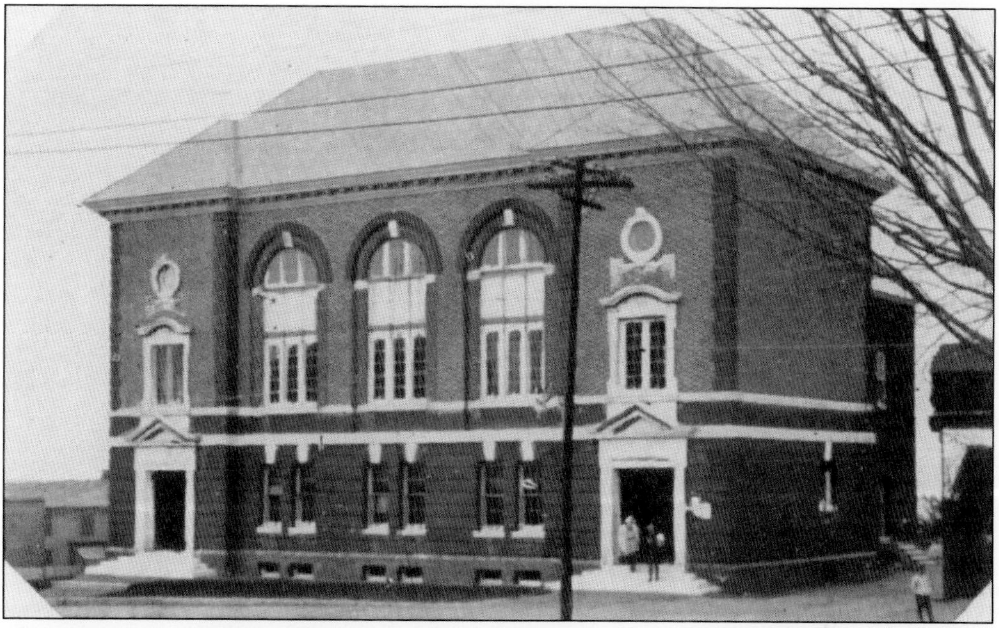

The present town hall on Main Street was opened in 1903, and the building was renovated in 1987.

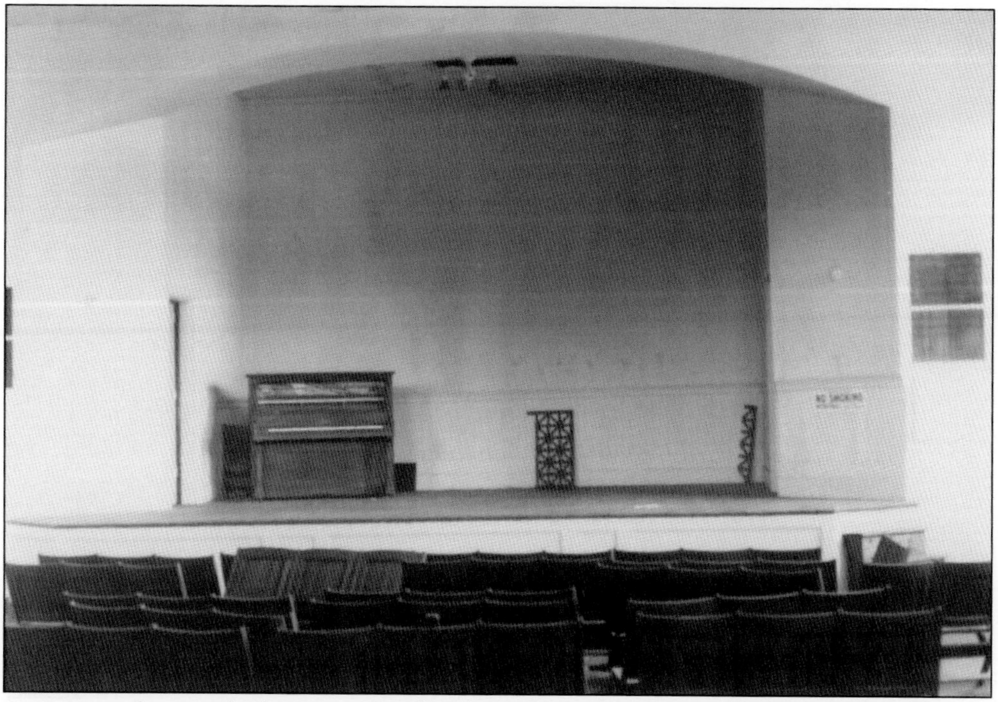

A piano on the town hall stage was used in the 1920s and 1930s for recitals and dances.

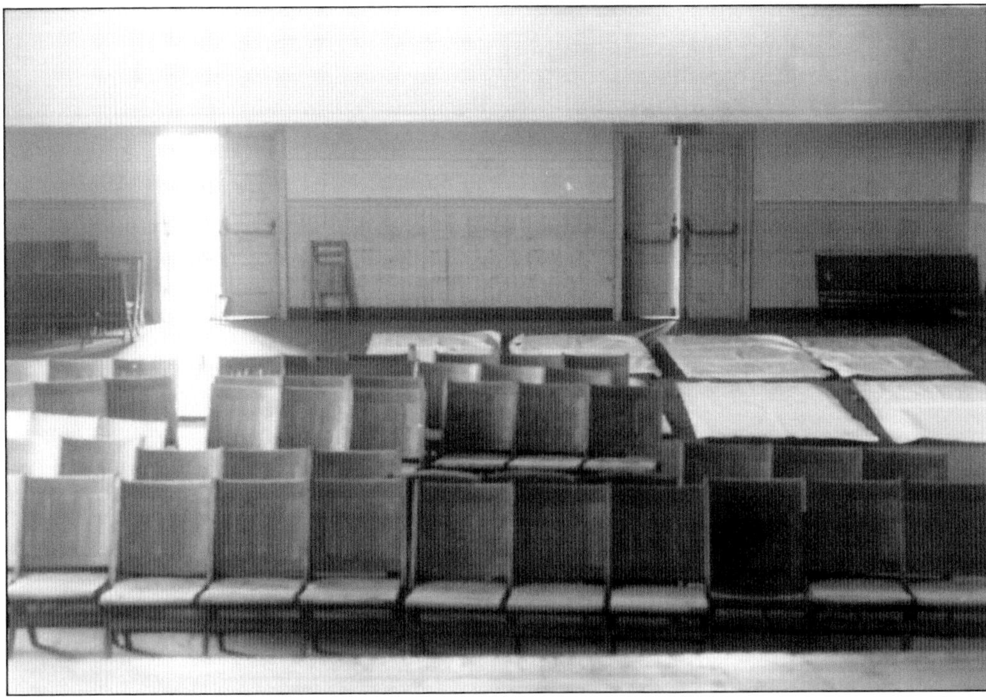

The town hall floor is shown prior to the renovation of the building in 1987.

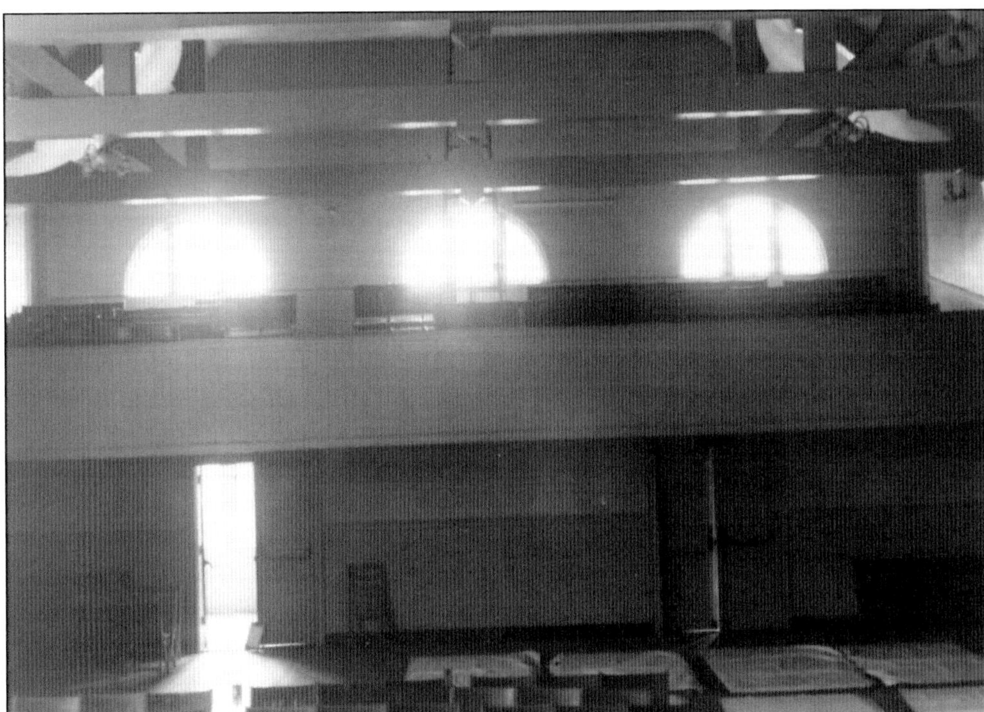

This view provides a look at the original rear balcony in the town hall.

Four

Churches and Cemeteries

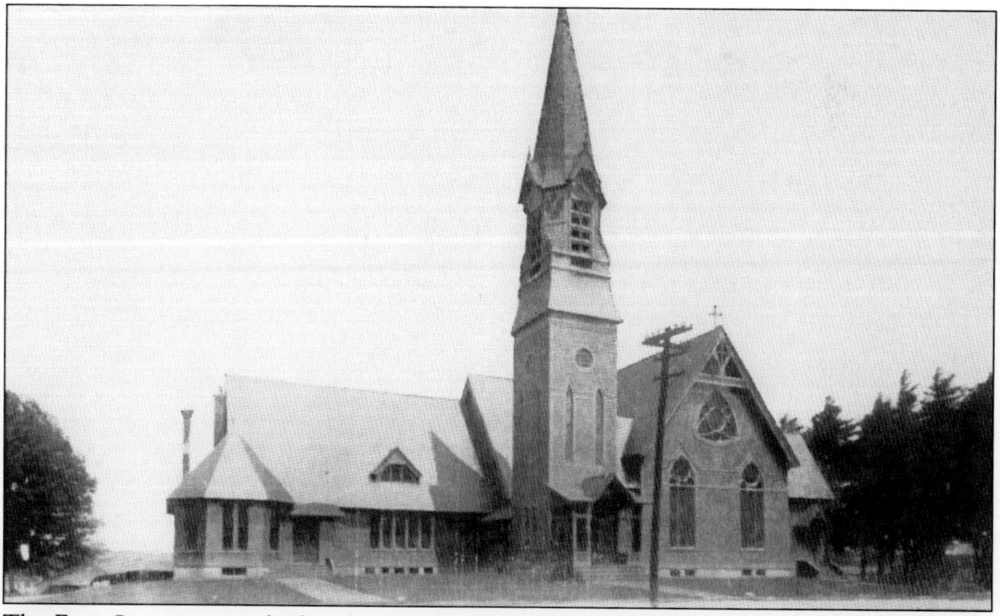

The First Congregational Church, once known as the third meetinghouse, was dedicated on May 9, 1883.

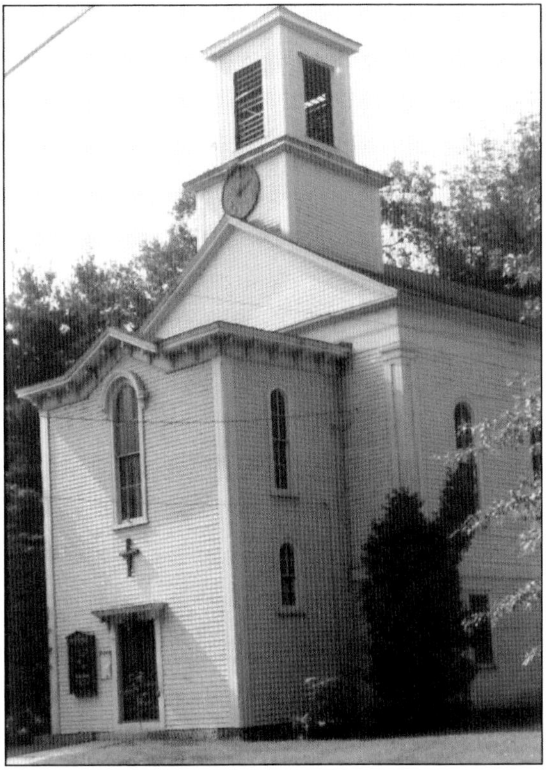

This Baptist church was located on Wood Street in Woodville from 1815 to 1995.

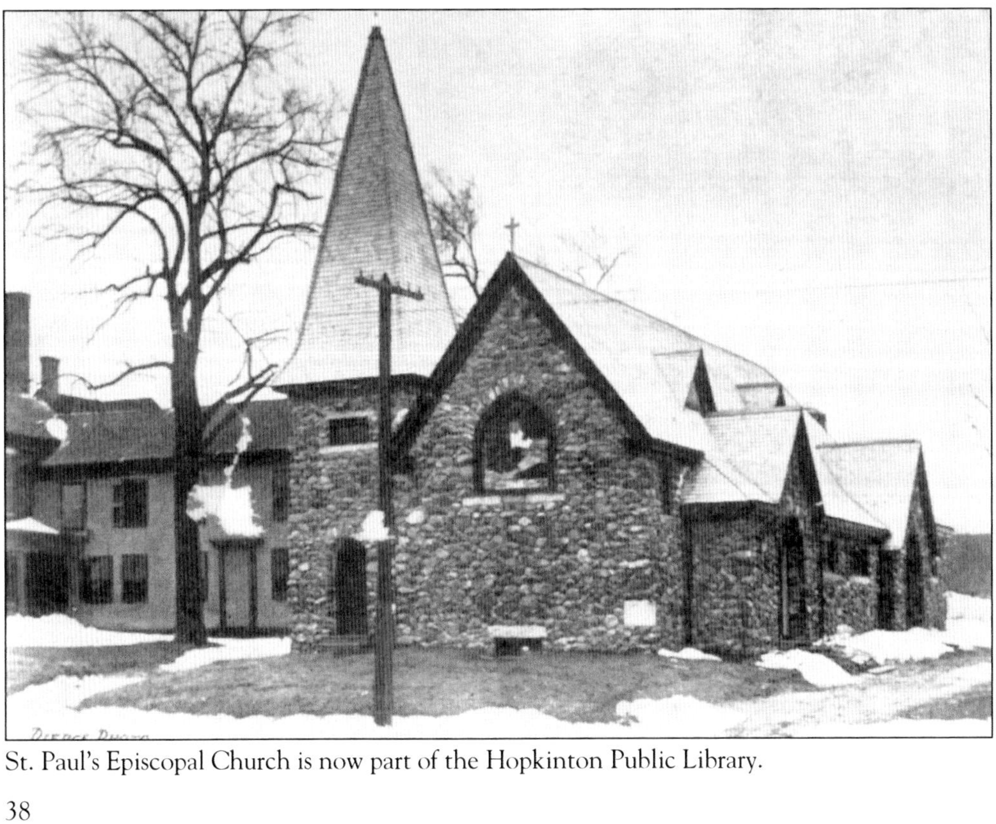

St. Paul's Episcopal Church is now part of the Hopkinton Public Library.

St. Malachi's Church was located on Cedar Street from 1851 to 1879. An addition was built to the structure in 1853. The church was built by Artemus Johnson of Hopkinton.

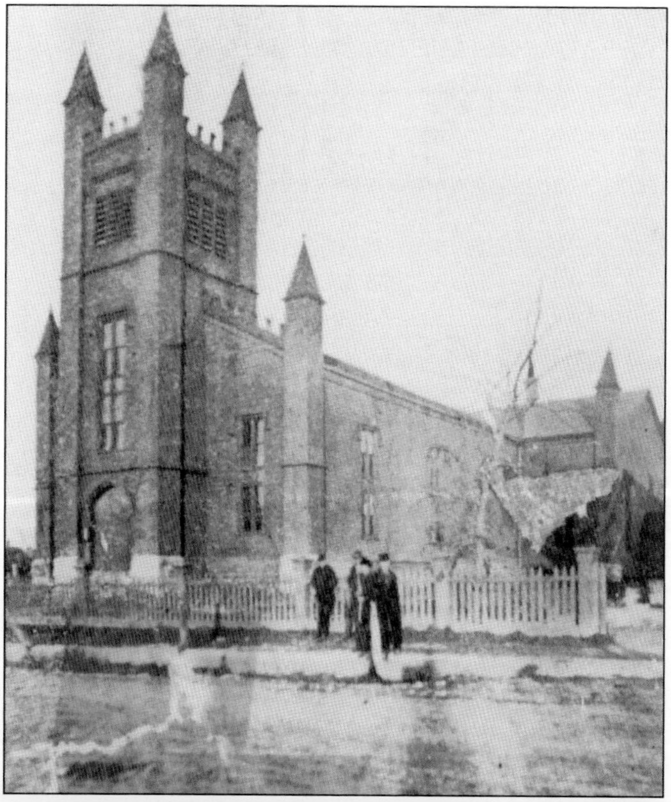

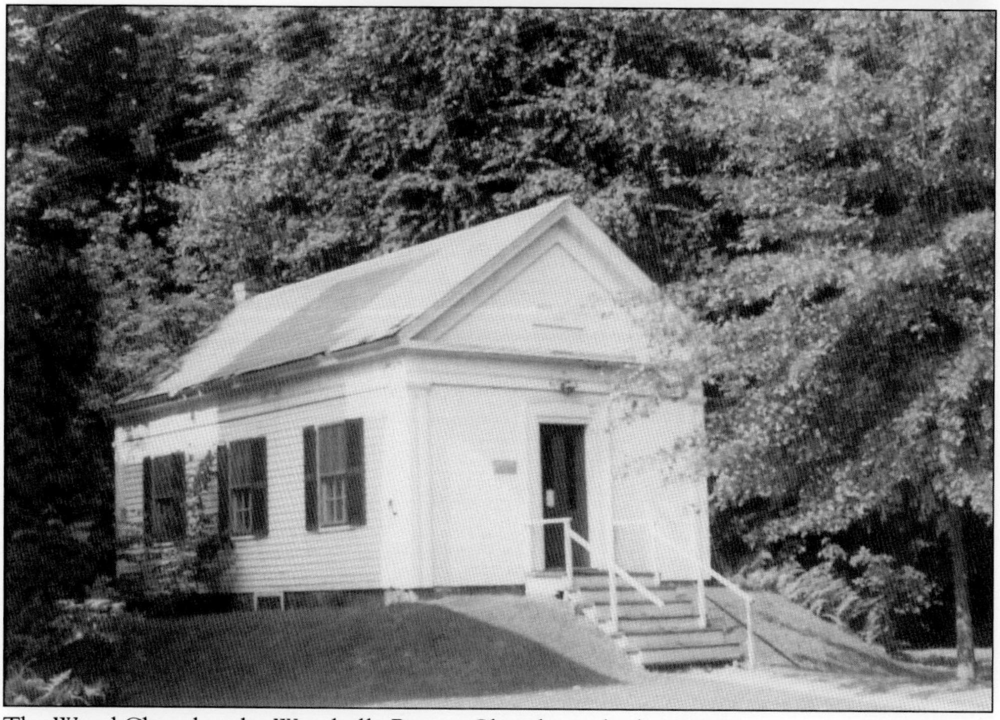

The Wood Chapel at the Woodville Baptist Church was built in 1866.

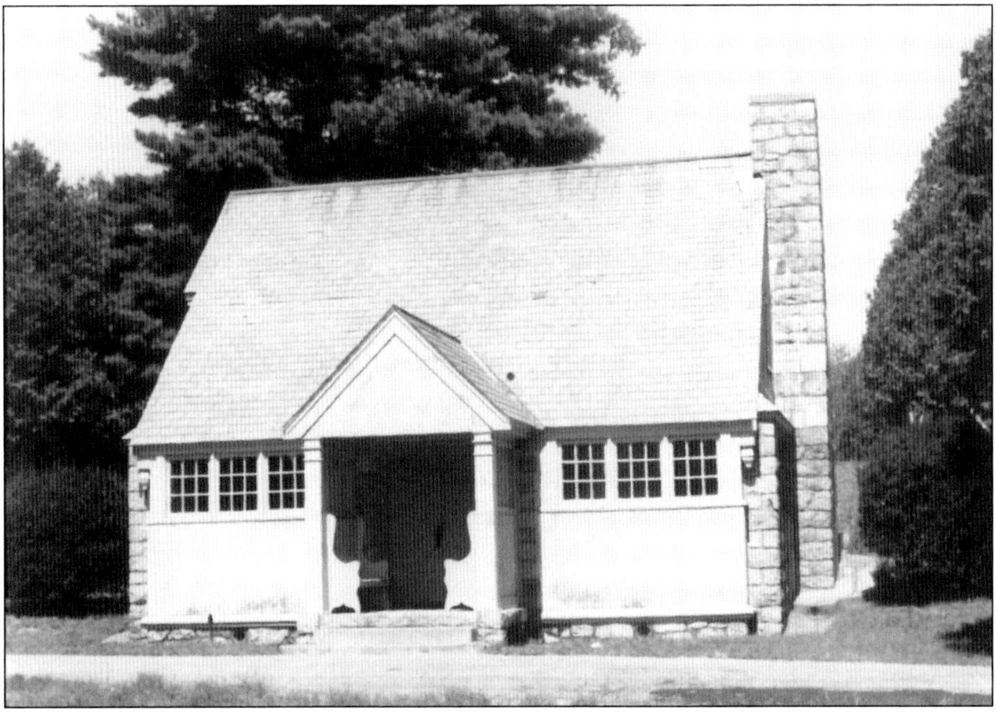

The Comey Memorial Chapel at Evergreen Cemetery is used occasionally for services. Note its fine chimney.

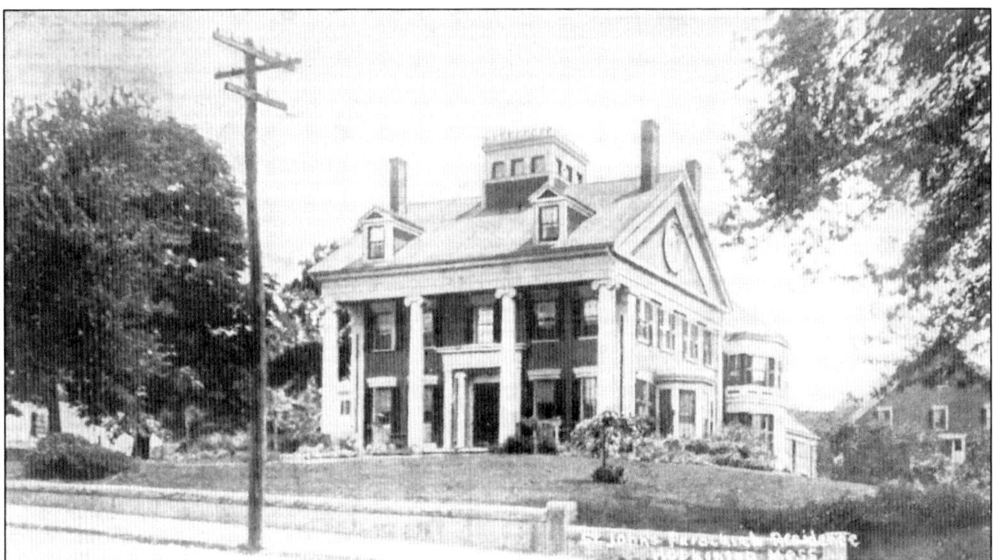

St. John's parochial residence on Main Street was replaced in 1995.

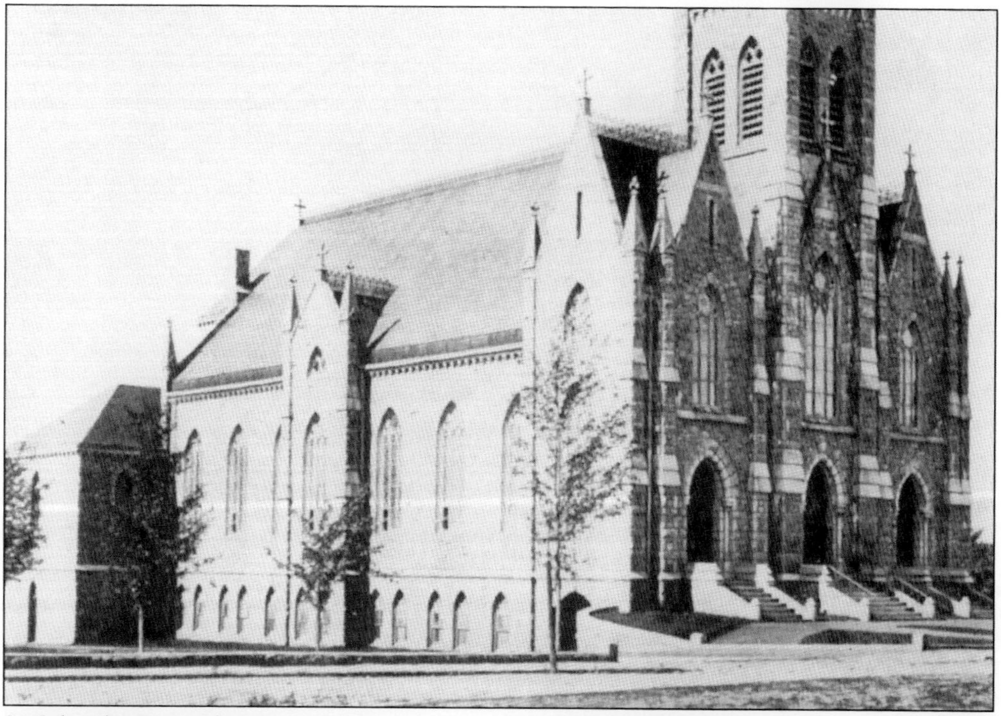

St. John the Evangelist Catholic Church was dedicated on September 2, 1889.

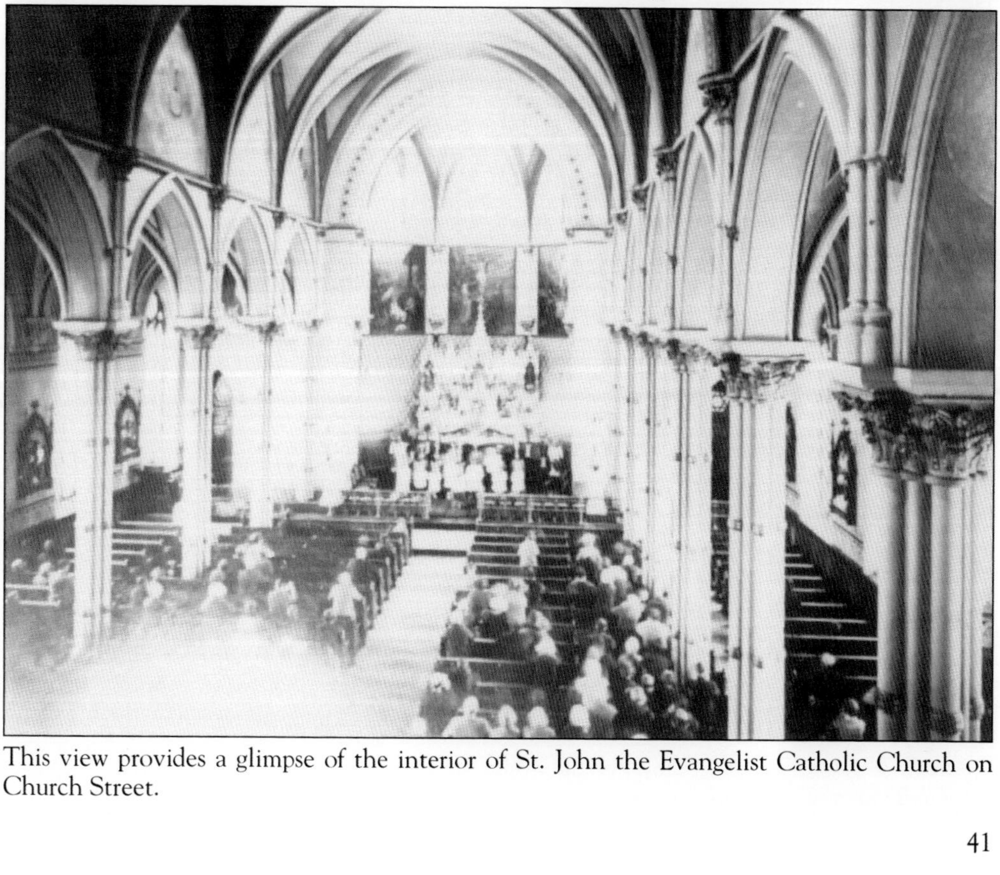

This view provides a glimpse of the interior of St. John the Evangelist Catholic Church on Church Street.

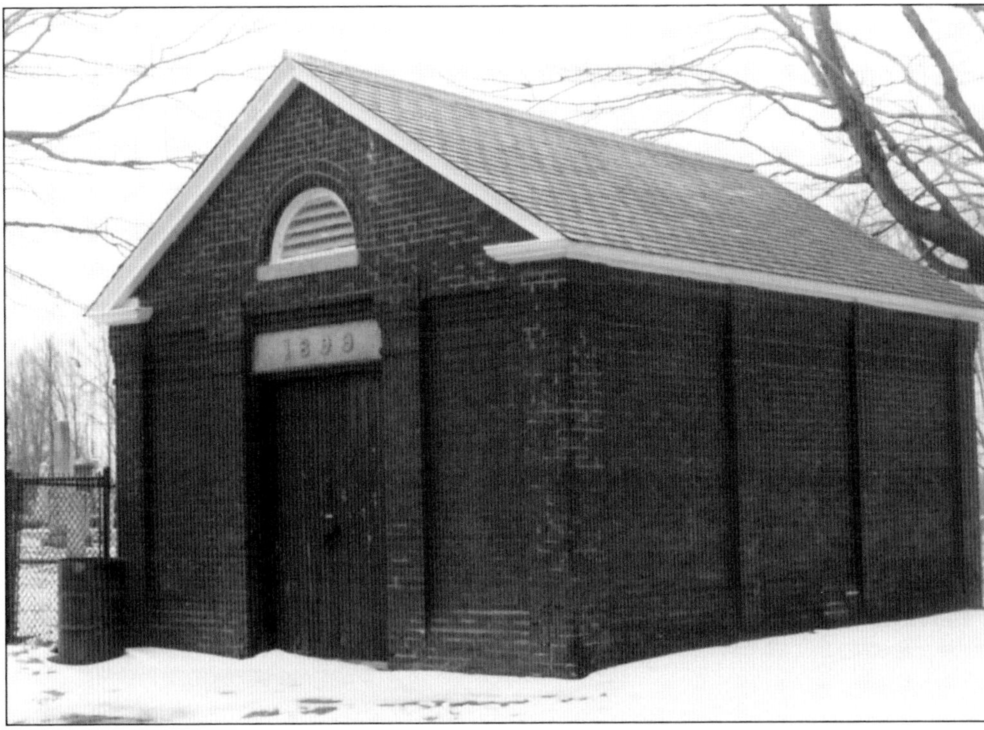

This brick tomb at Mt. Auburn Cemetery was built in 1898.

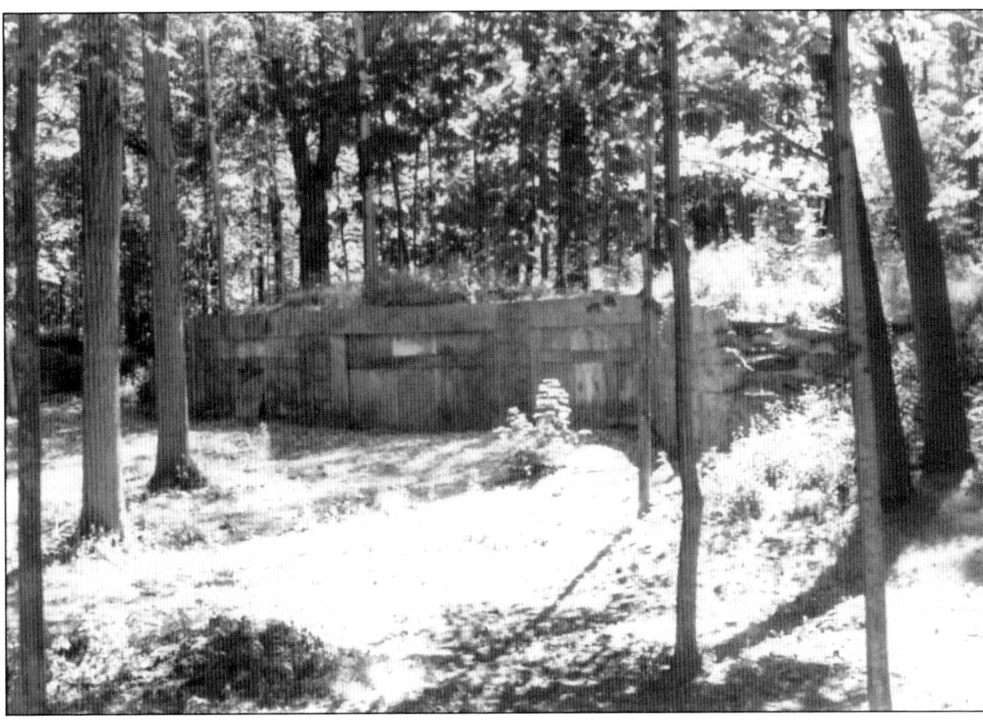

A portion of the abandoned "Tombs" on East Main Street is an old private burial ground belonging to a family named Valentine. Sometimes, this area is called the Washburn Cemetery.

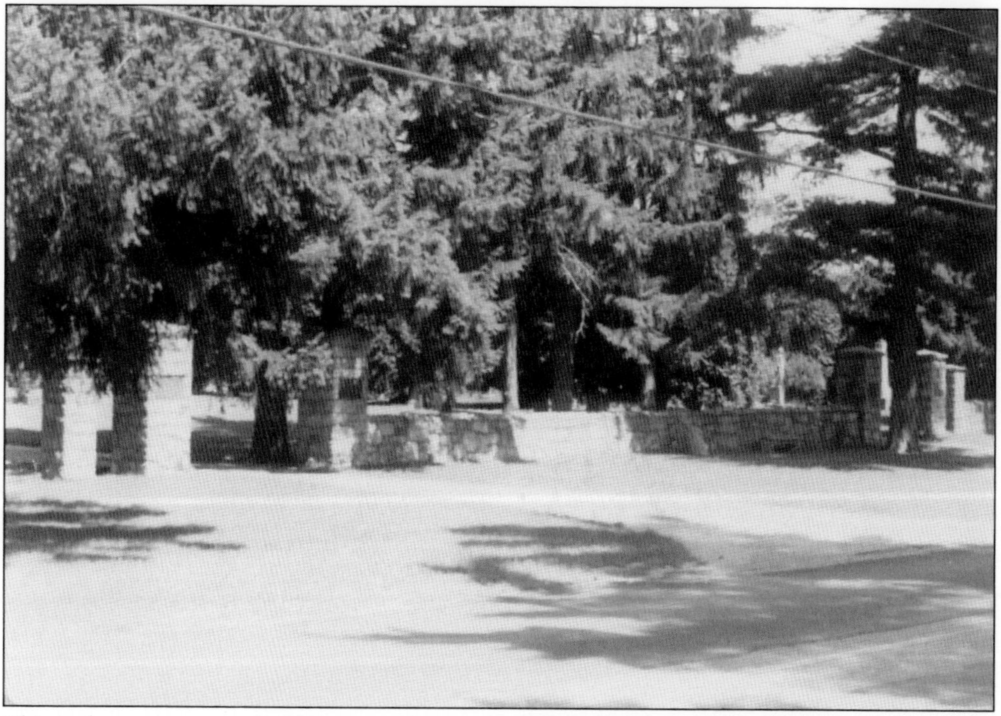

This is the entrance to the Evergreen Cemetery on Wood Street in Woodville.

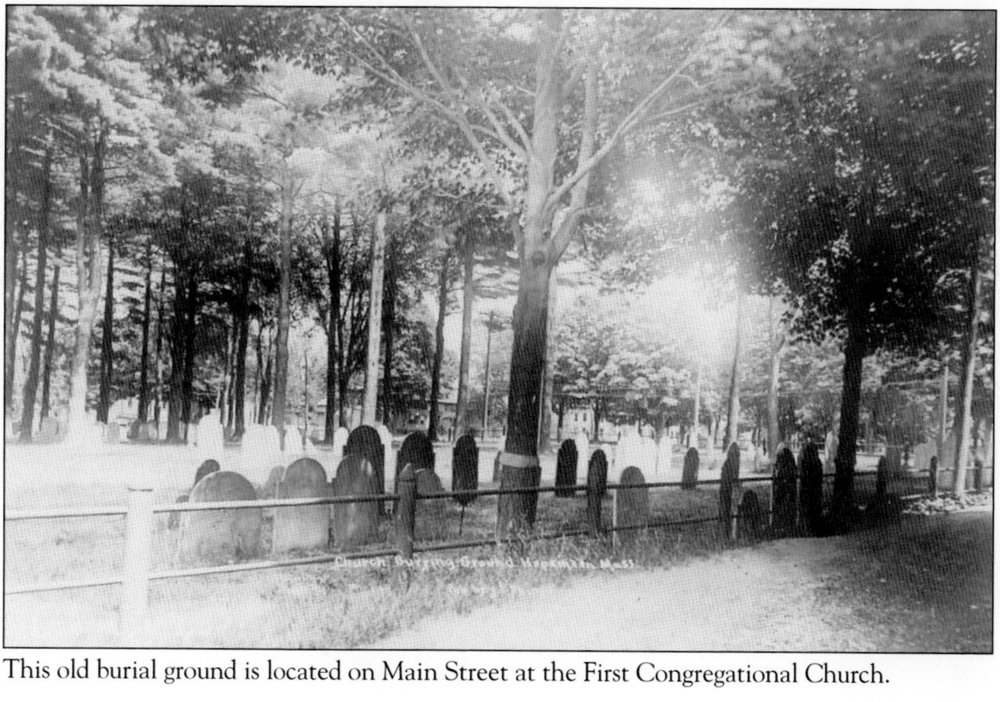

This old burial ground is located on Main Street at the First Congregational Church.

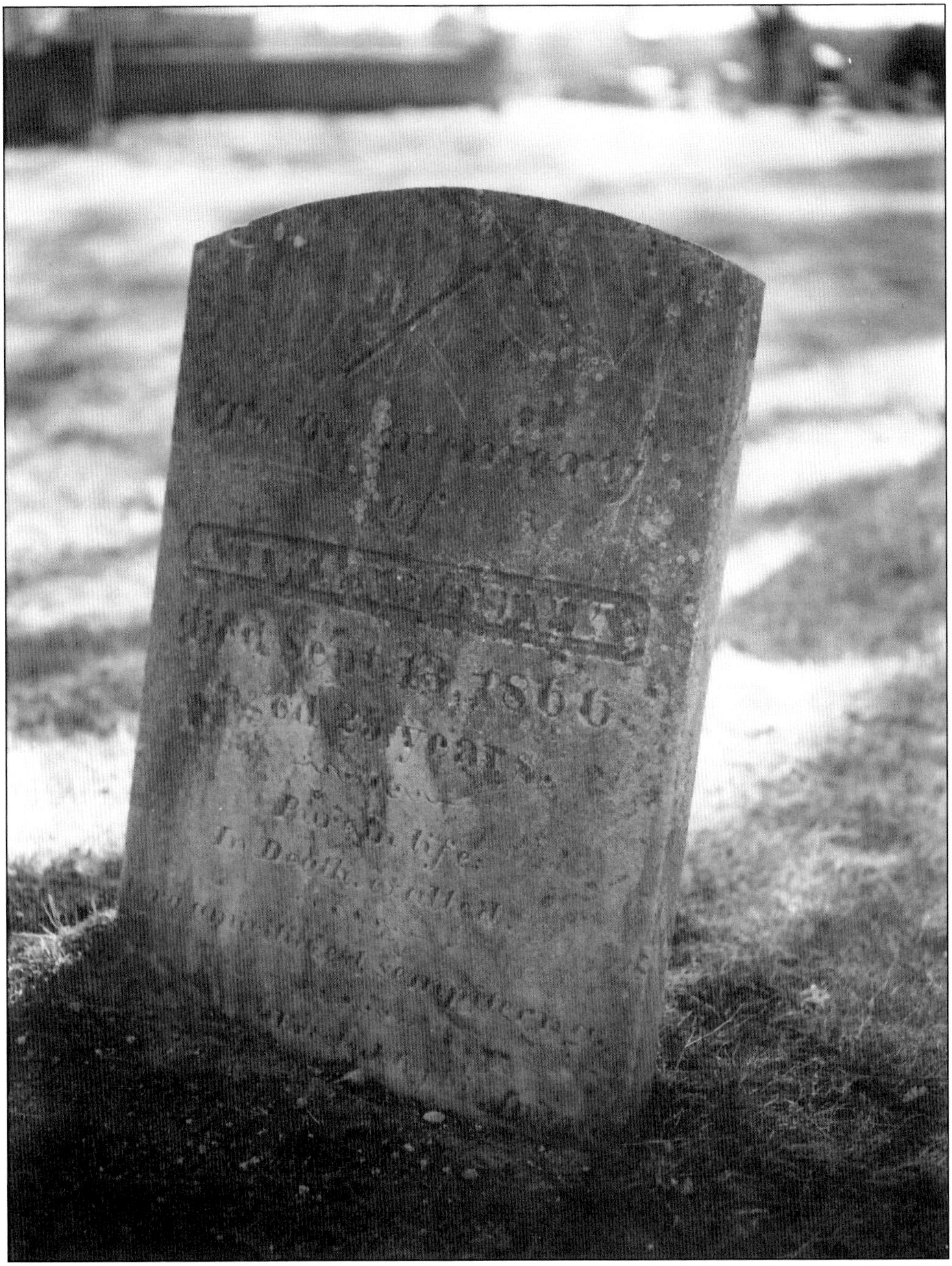

The grave of Ahwanetunk, a Native American, is located at Mt. Auburn Cemetery. He died in Hopkinton while working for a traveling circus on September 13, 1886. The monument was erected by his friend, E.S. Washburn.

Five

Buildings

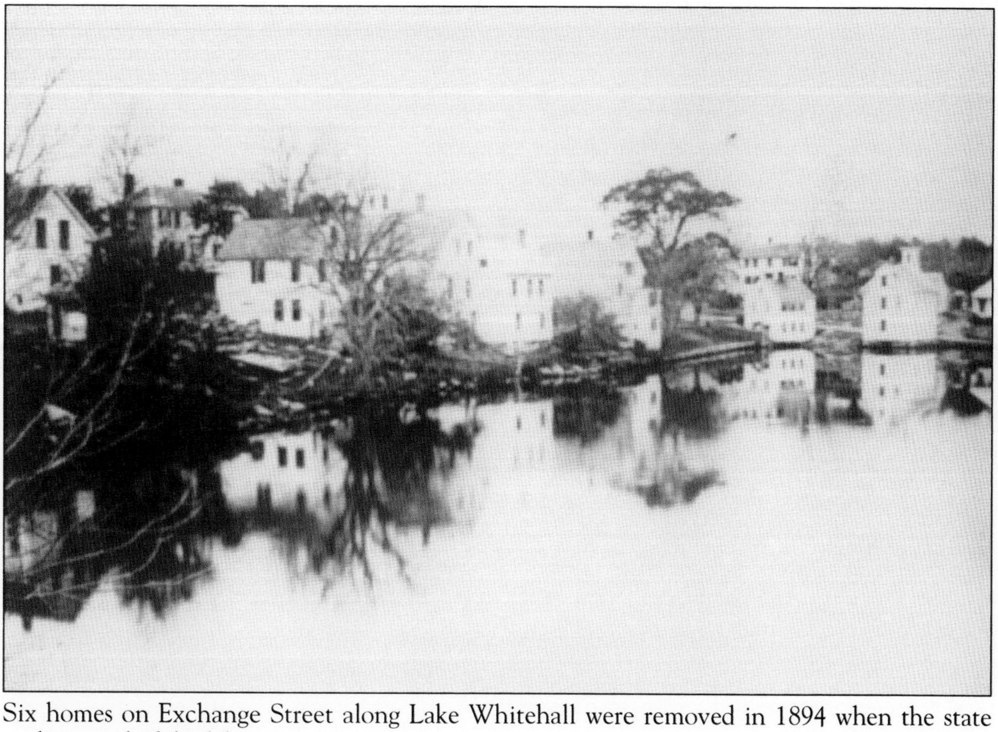

Six homes on Exchange Street along Lake Whitehall were removed in 1894 when the state took control of the lake.

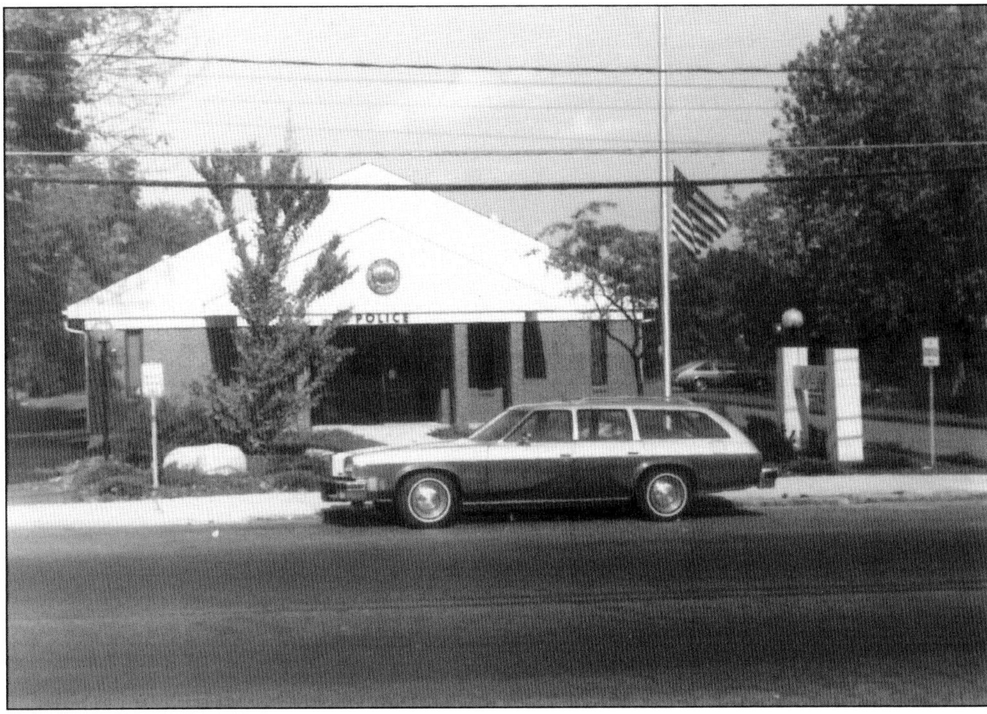

The Hopkinton's police station was built around 1980 on Main Street.

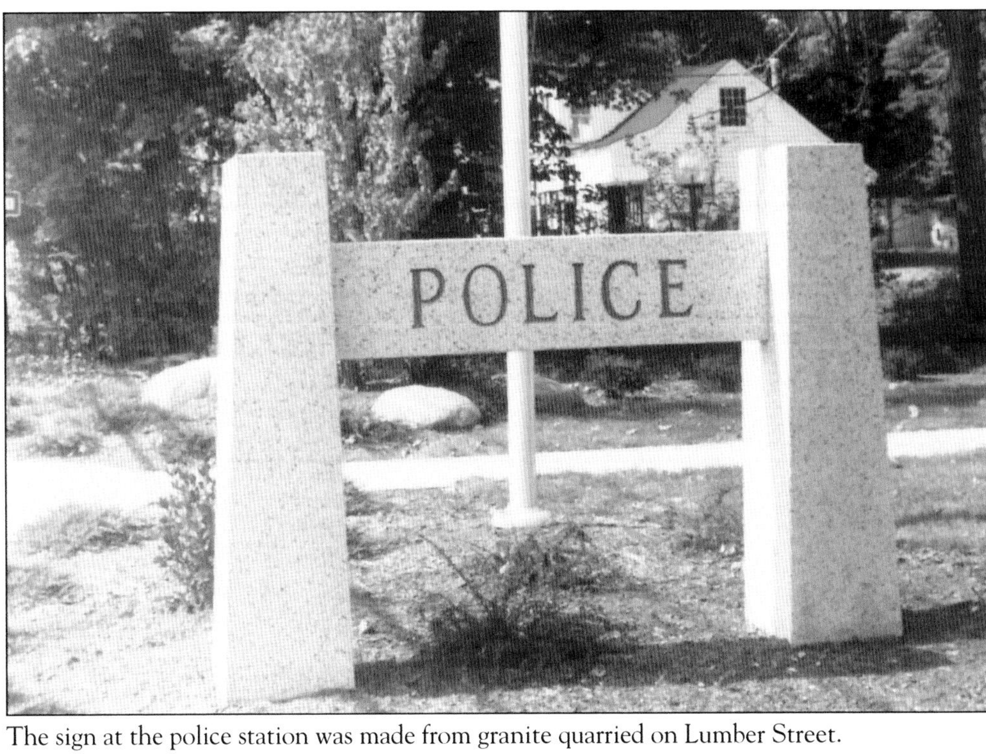

The sign at the police station was made from granite quarried on Lumber Street.

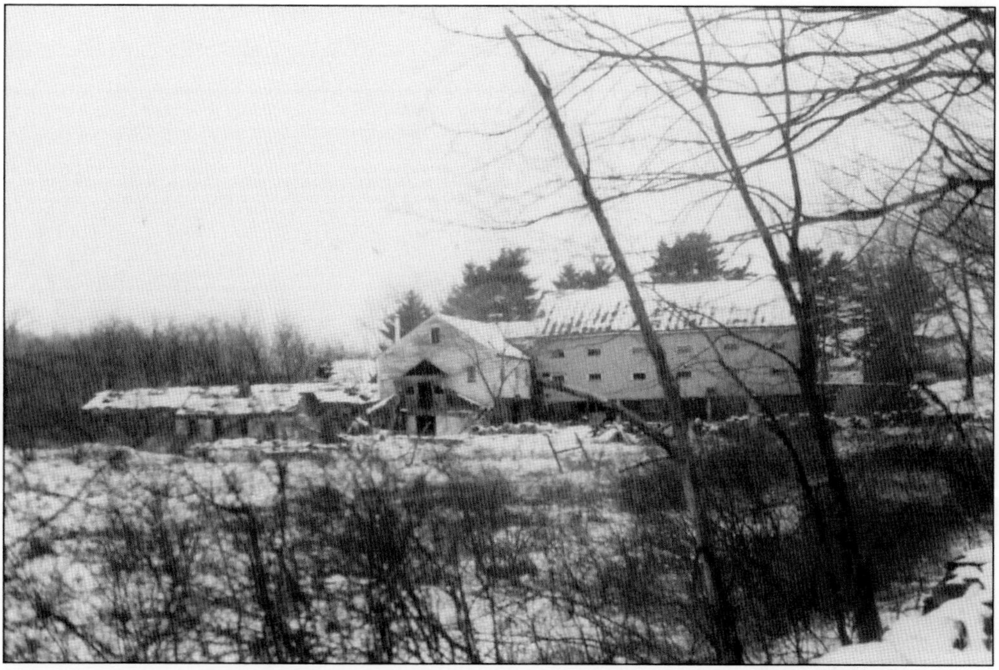

Now the site of several new homes, the former Beckford farm stood at 155 Fruit Street.

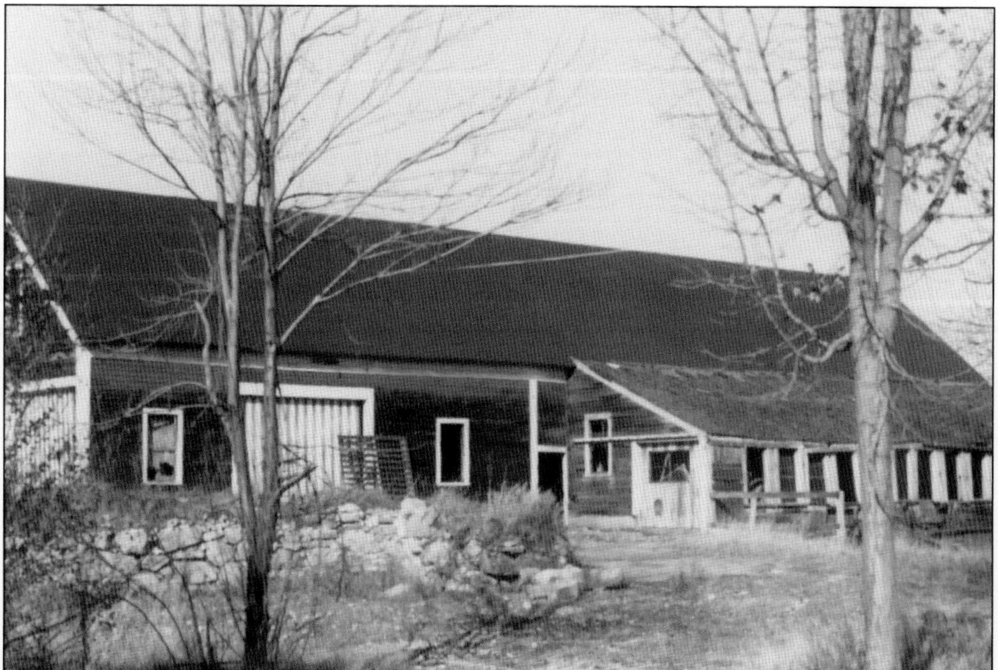

Creedan's barn was located near the intersection of Elm and Wood Streets in 1940.

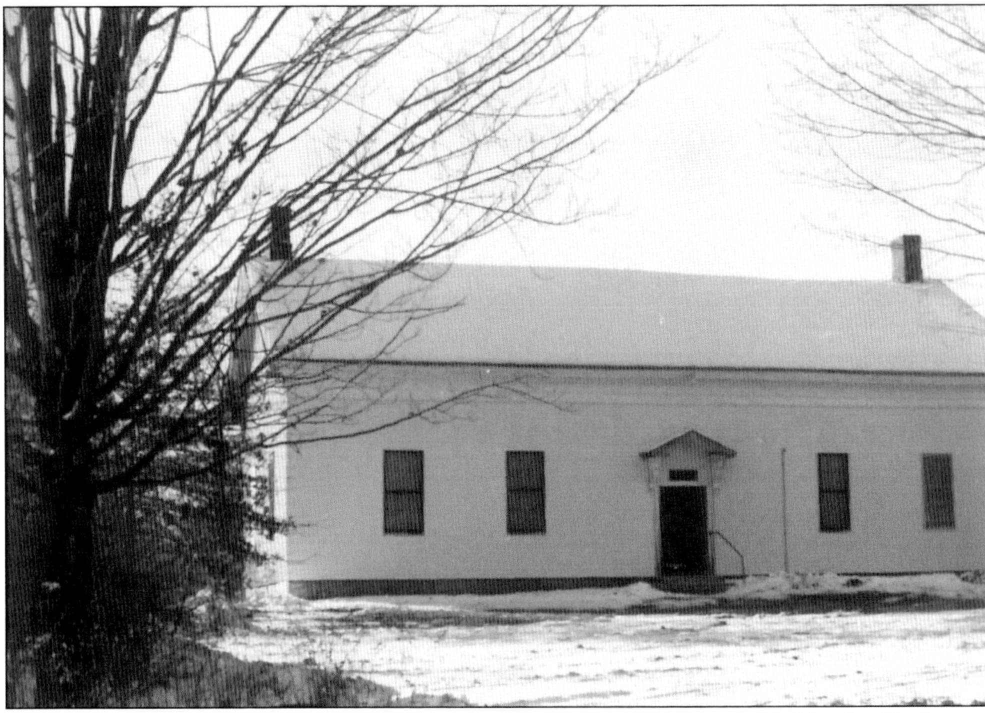

Hopkinton Grange No. 173, located on Hayden Rowe Street, is now owned by the Hopkinton Historical Society.

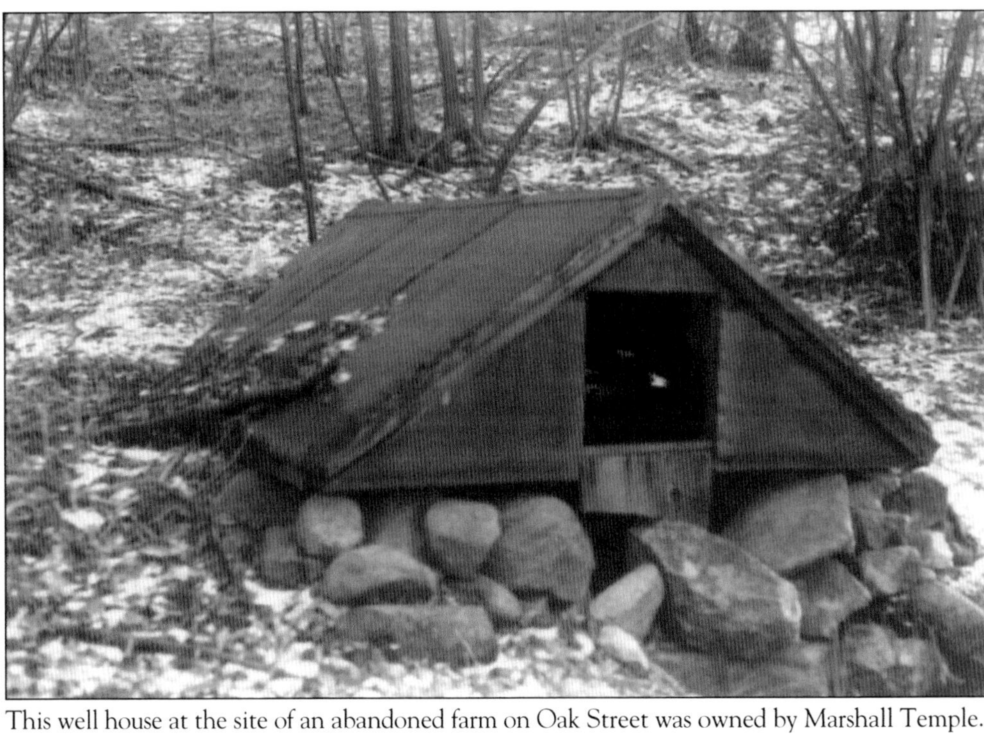

This well house at the site of an abandoned farm on Oak Street was owned by Marshall Temple.

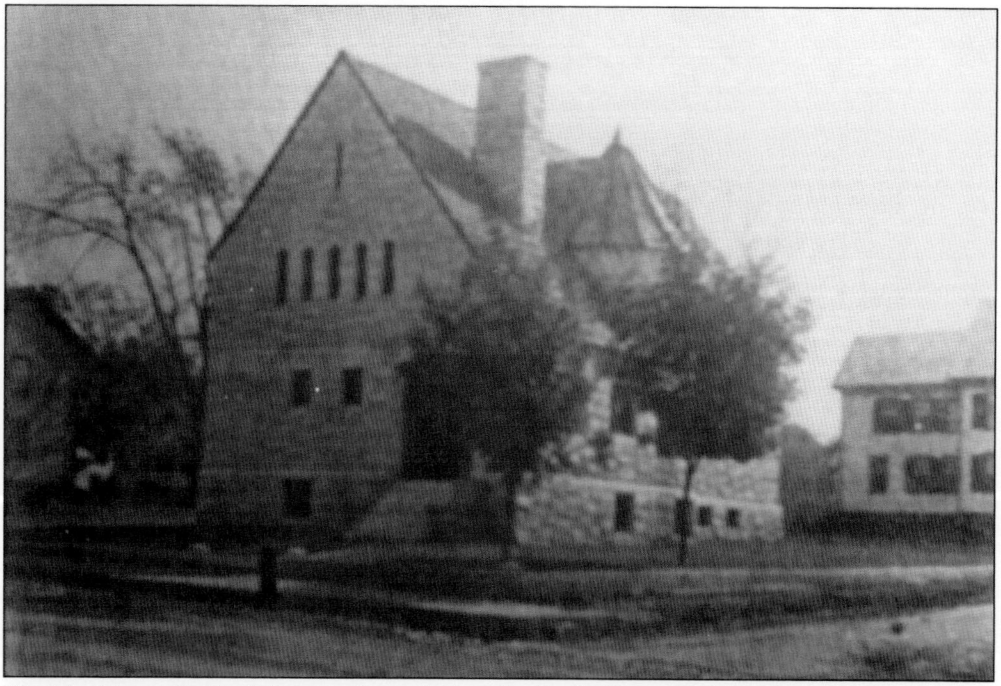

The Hopkinton Public Library is shown before St. Paul's Episcopal Church was built.

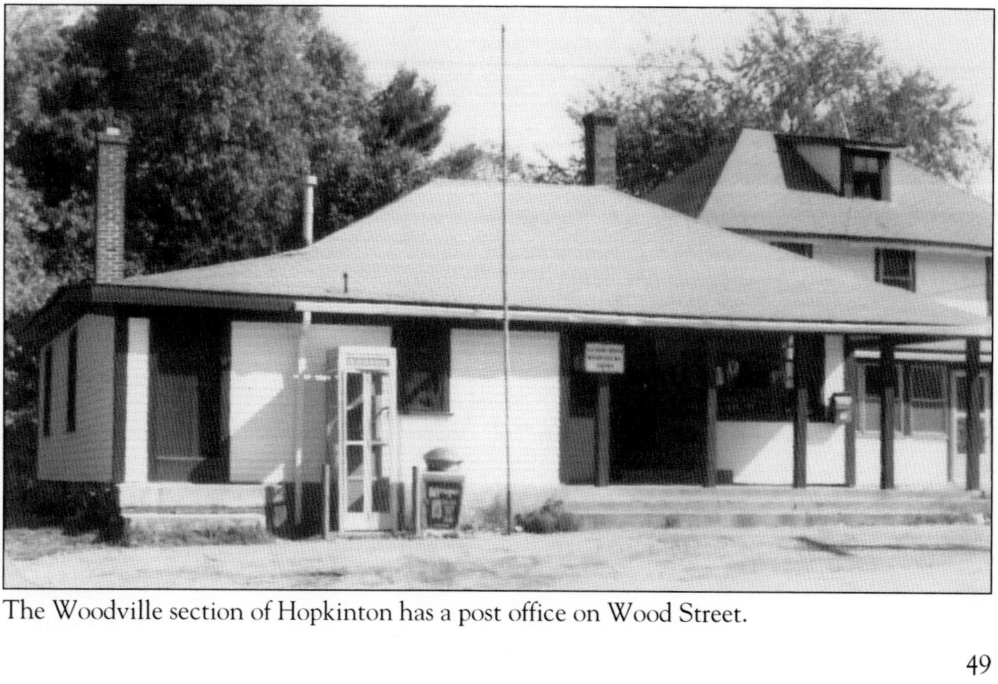

The Woodville section of Hopkinton has a post office on Wood Street.

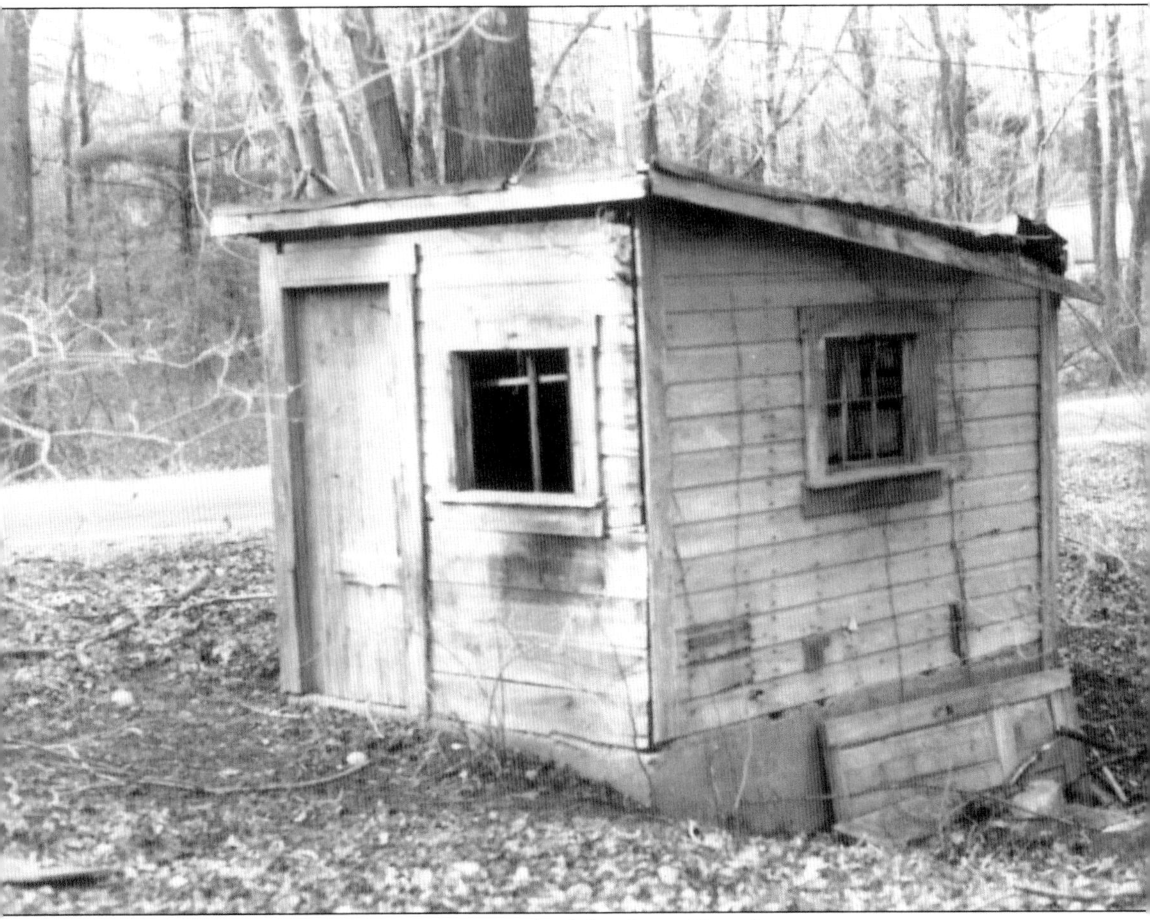

This well house at 107 Spring Street was built by Oscar Temple.

Six

People and Houses

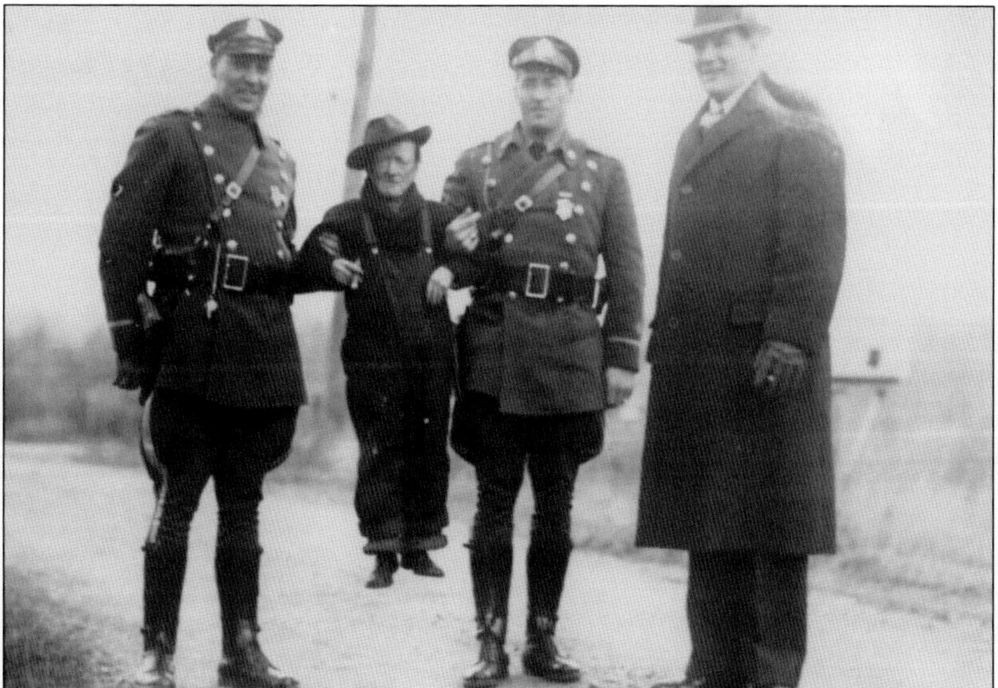

A few of Hopkinton's well-known residents gathered for this photograph. From left to right, individuals pictured are as follows: State Trooper William Blusteen, Michael Maloney (a well-known midget who lived and worked in Hopkinton), and State Trooper Stanley Schilling. The man on the far right is Hopkinton Police Chief Edward V. McManus. Maloney was 36 or 40 inches tall when he was forty years old.

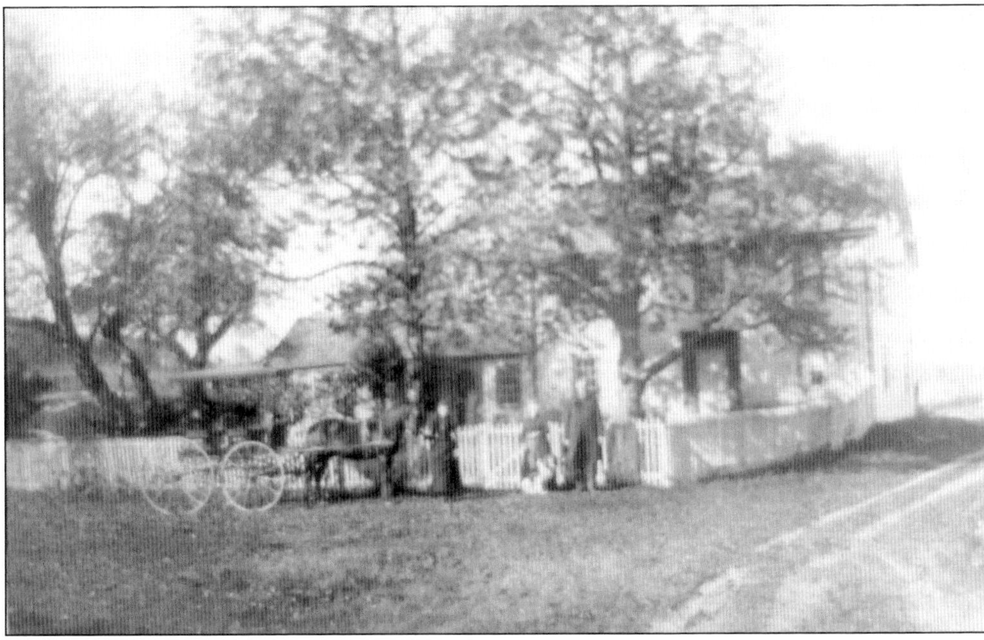

The Nathan Doubleday home was on West Street, as shown in this 1887 photograph. This site is now under the Hopkinton Reservoir.

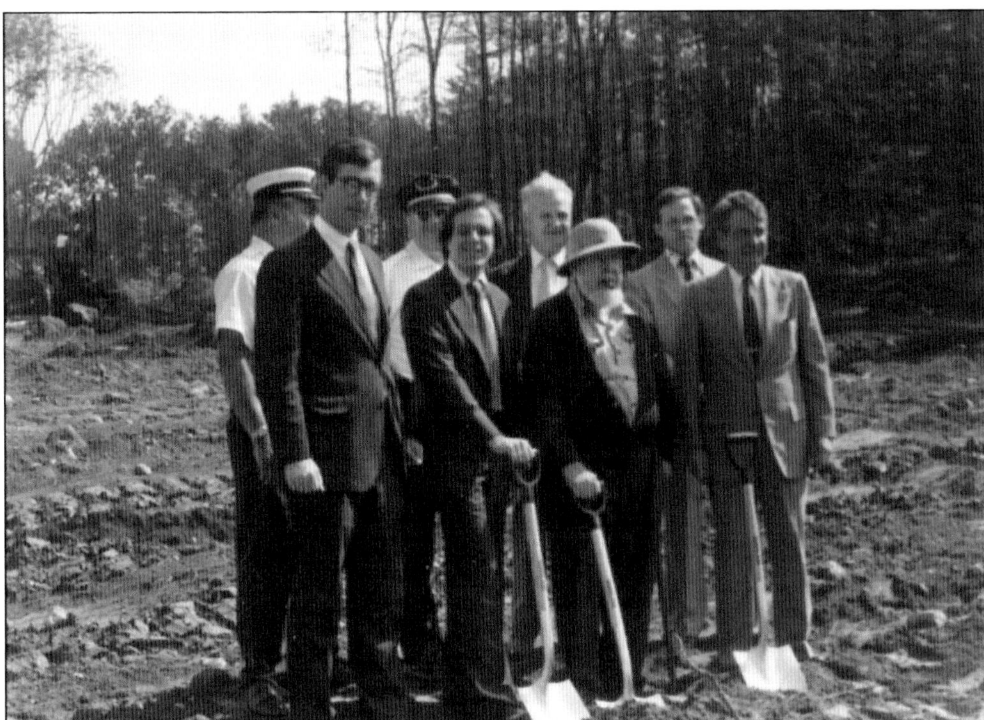

Ground-breaking ceremonies were held in September 1981 for the Hopkinton Office and Research Park. The photograph includes Fire Chief Arthur Stewart, Police Chief Jerry Bowker, Ernest Fecteau, Selectman John Hinckley, and Nelson McIntire.

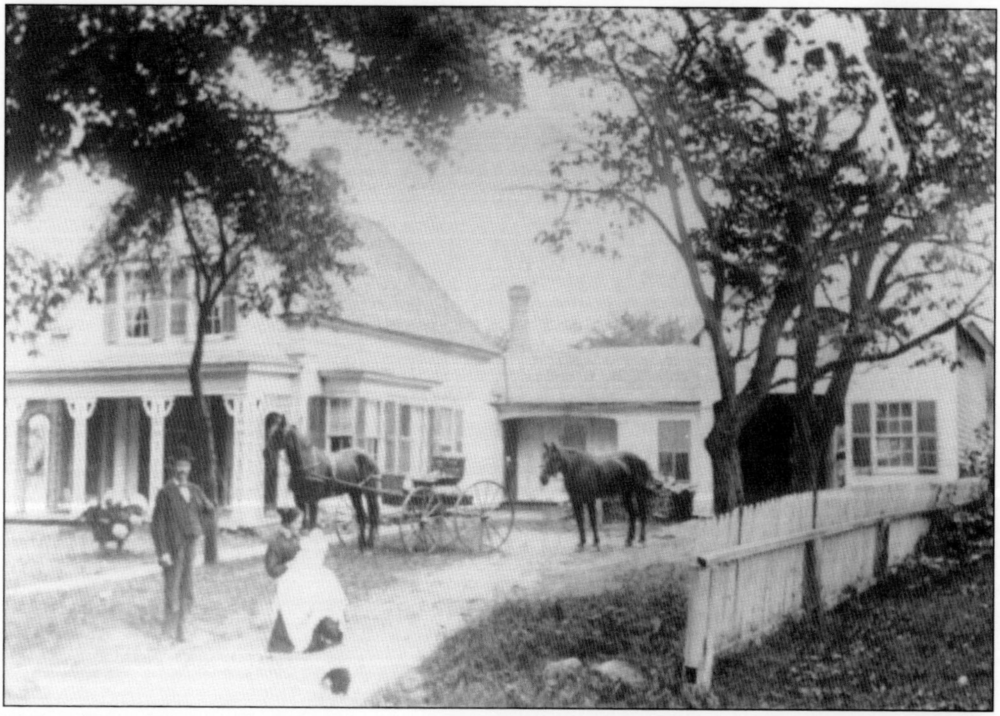

Mr. and Mrs. Thomas F. Callanan were photographed at their home on Hayden Rowe Street. The baby is Francis Callanan.

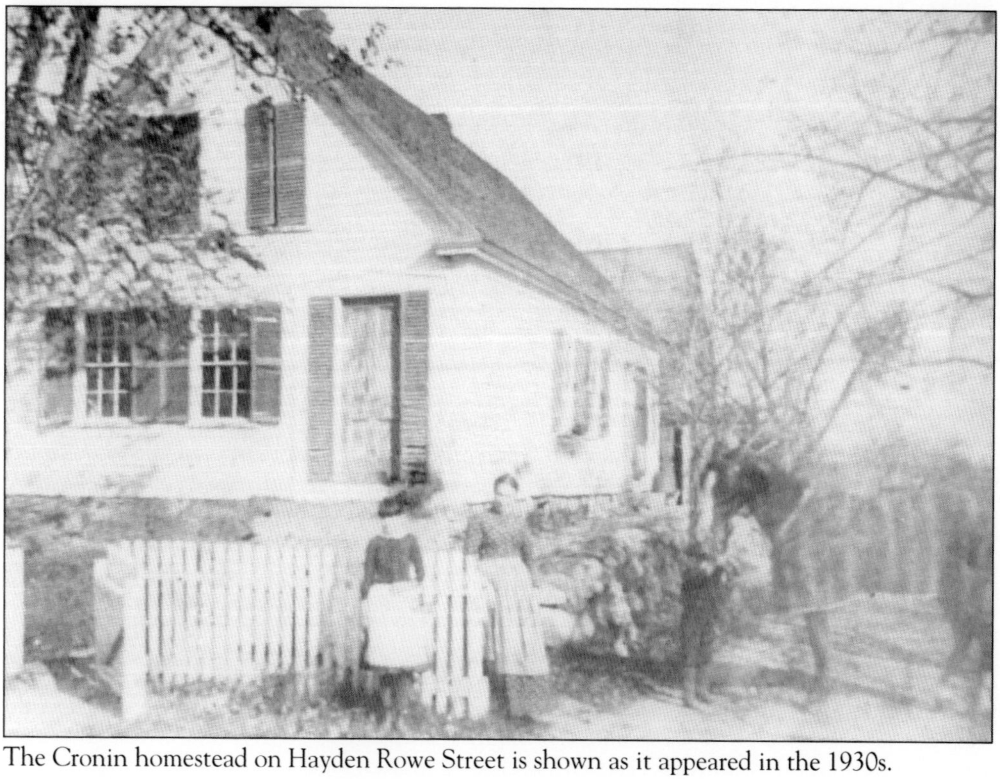

The Cronin homestead on Hayden Rowe Street is shown as it appeared in the 1930s.

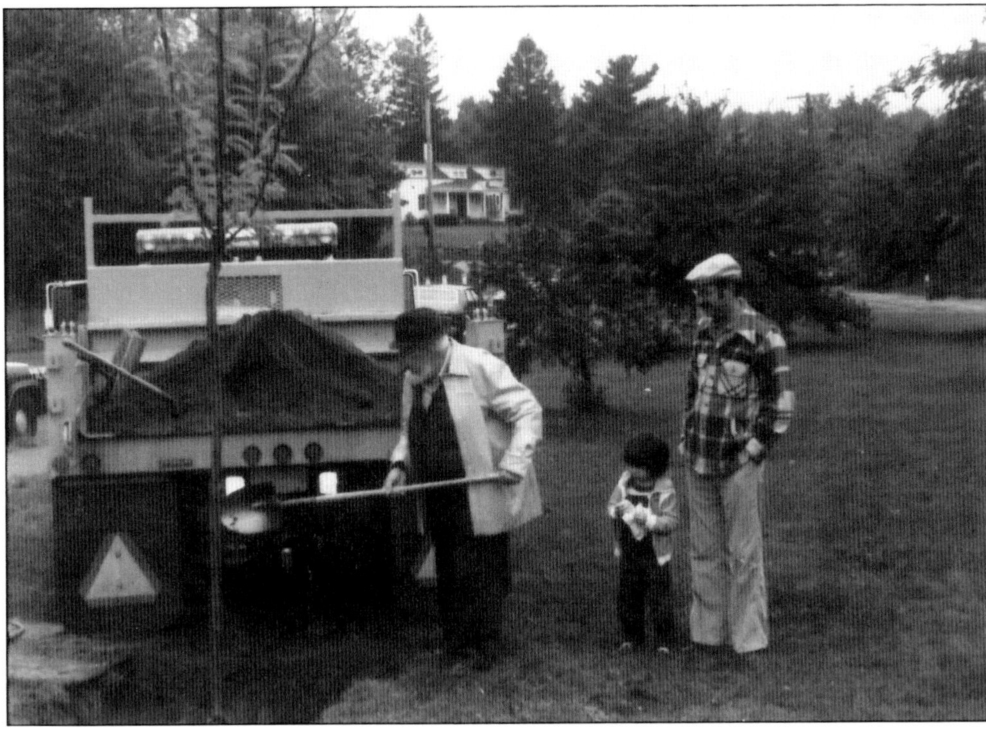

Nelson McIntire (left) plants a memorial tree on Wood Street. The others are state representative Andrew Natsios and his son.

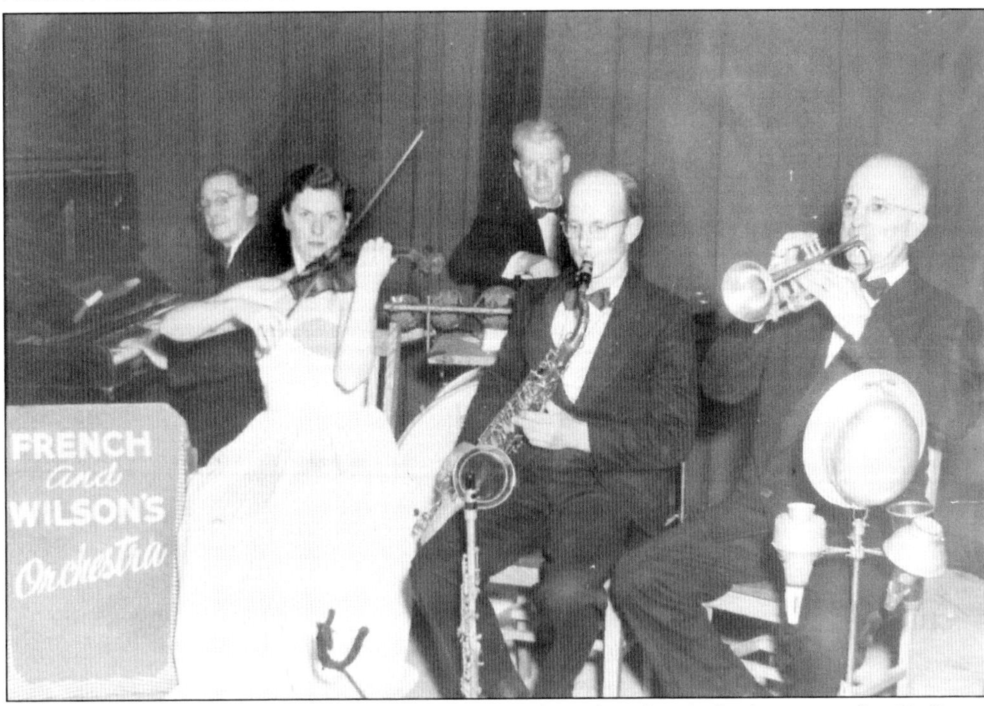

Russ Stratton is playing his saxophone with French and Wilson's Orchestra at the Holliston Town Hall. Russ had his own orchestra which played in the Hopkinton area for many years.

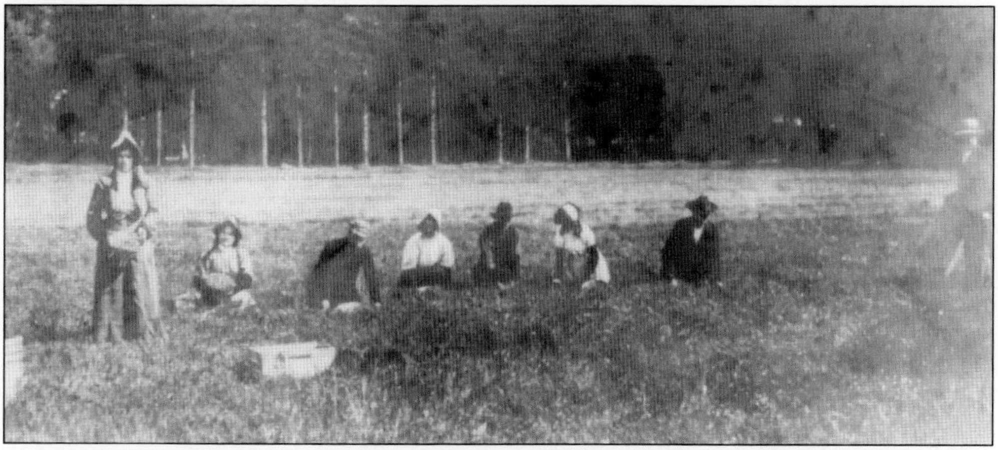

These people were harvesting cranberries for W.B. Claflin in 1920s. Workers, from left to right, are as follows: Vezee Higgins, Mrs. Benson, Melvin Cheney, Amy F. Stearns, Harry A. Cheney, Mrs. Cheney, Fred Albee, and Henry Sanger (far right).

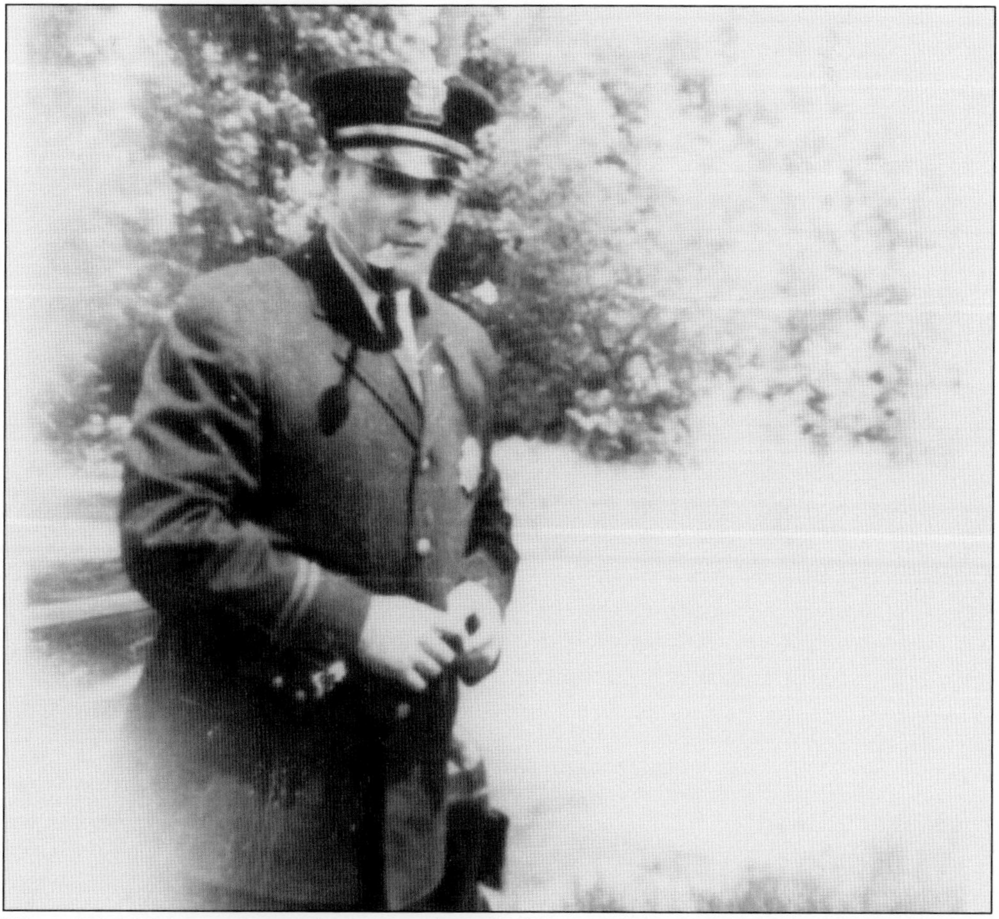

Edward V. McManus was Hopkinton's police chief from 1927 to 1945. He was also a foreman at Seaman & Cobb's. He died on May 22, 1984.

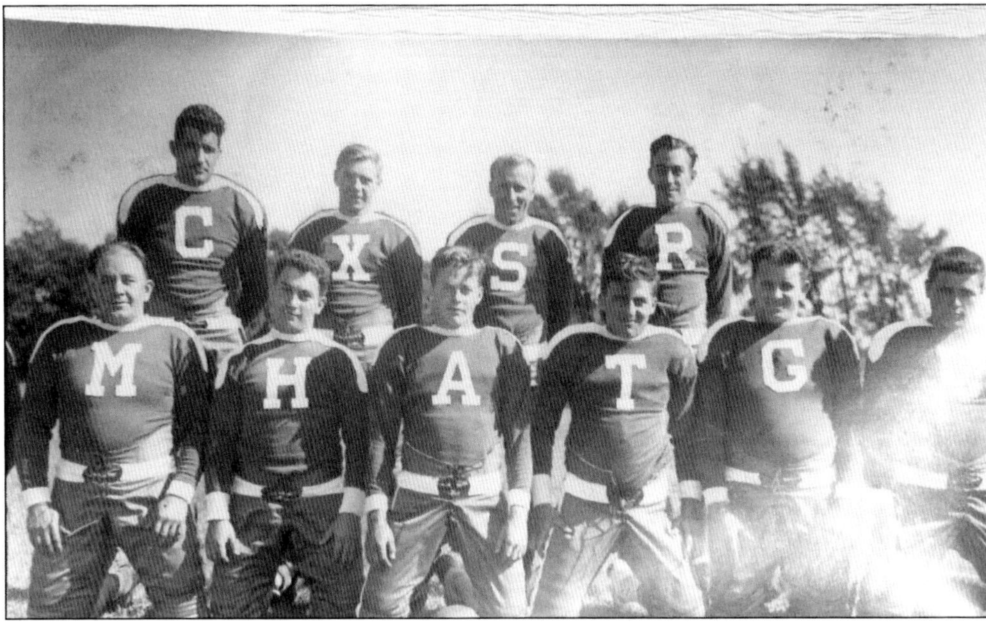

The members of the Hopkinton Stonethrowers football team posed for this team picture on September 13, 1938.

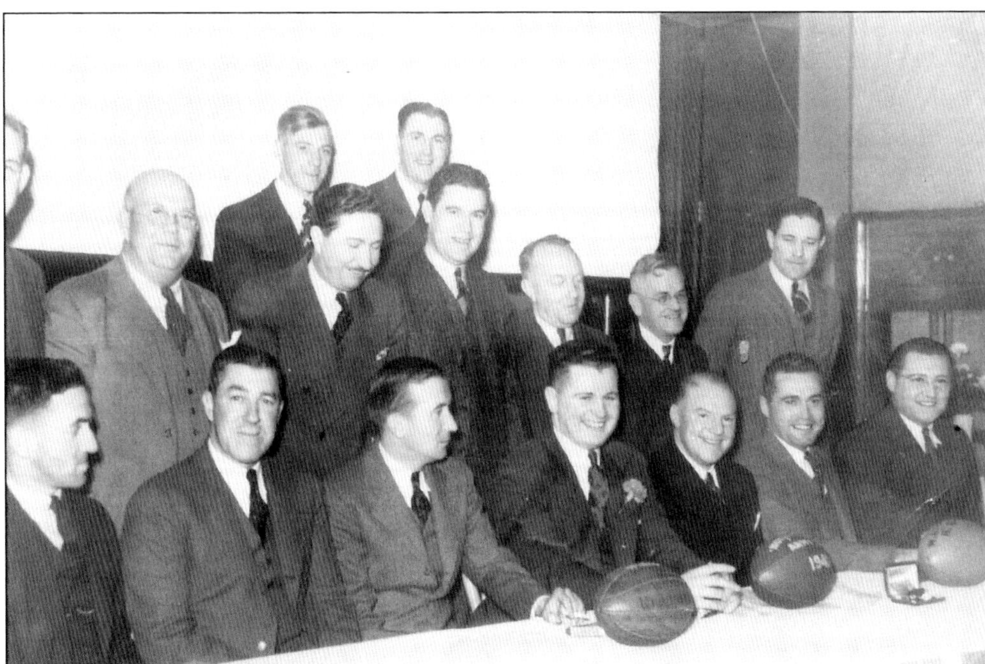

Former Hopkinton Stonethrowers honored Coach Welch on December 18, 1940. The footballs were used in 1940.

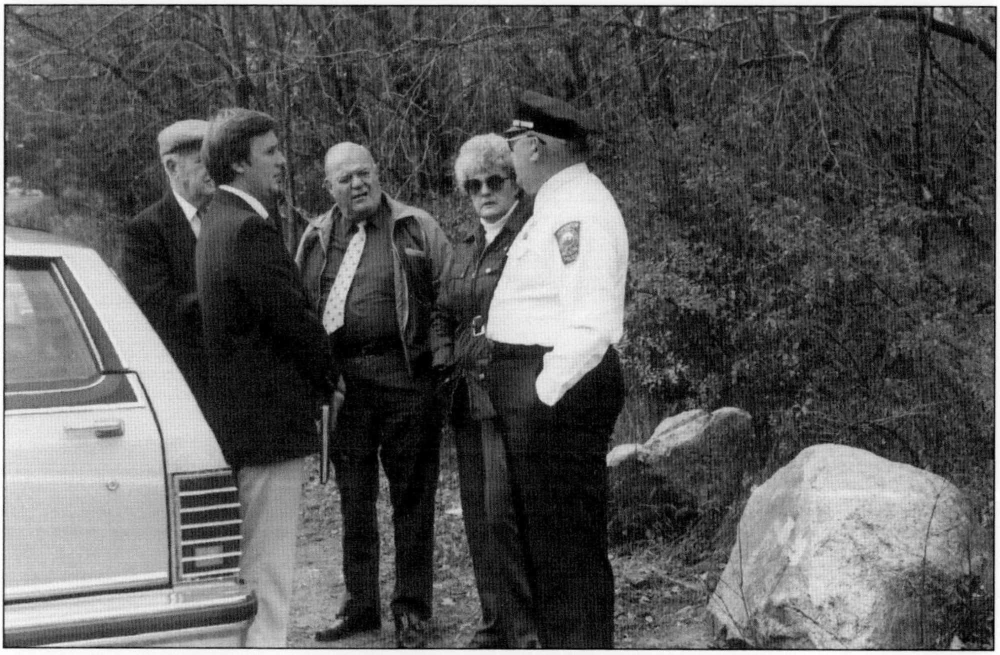

Town officials discuss the future location of a sign relating to the Hopkinton Industrial Park in 1981. From left to right are Ernest Fecteau, Jack McCarthy (of the State Department of Commerce), Selectman Alverie Paradis, Selectman Sallyann MacIntosh, and Police Chief Jerry Bowker.

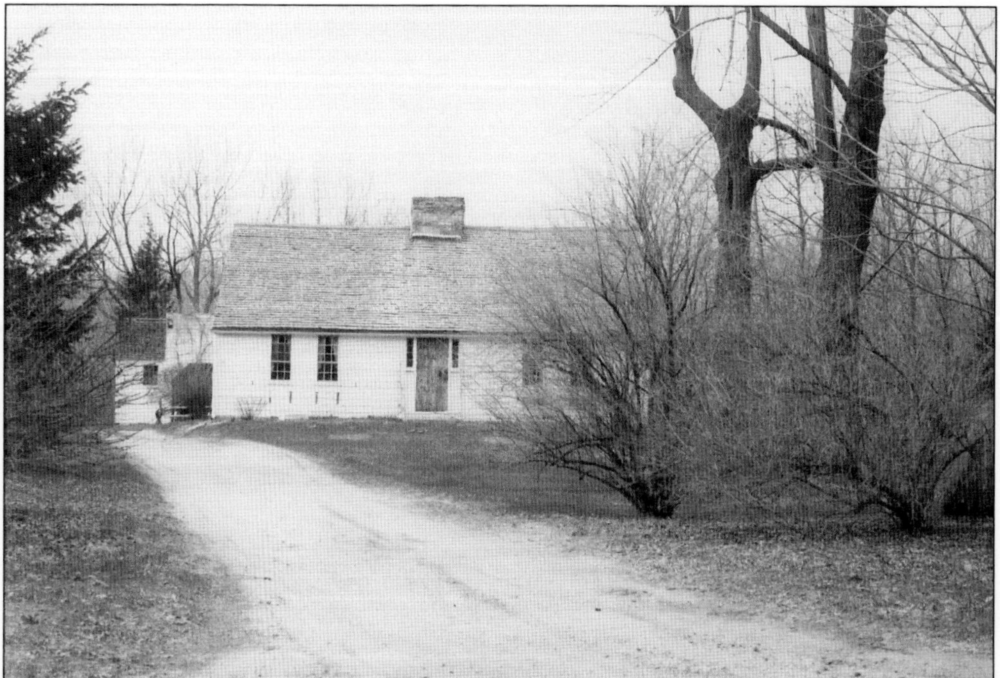

The J. Howard Leman farm, at 110 Pond Street, is the present site of the old Hopkinton railroad station.

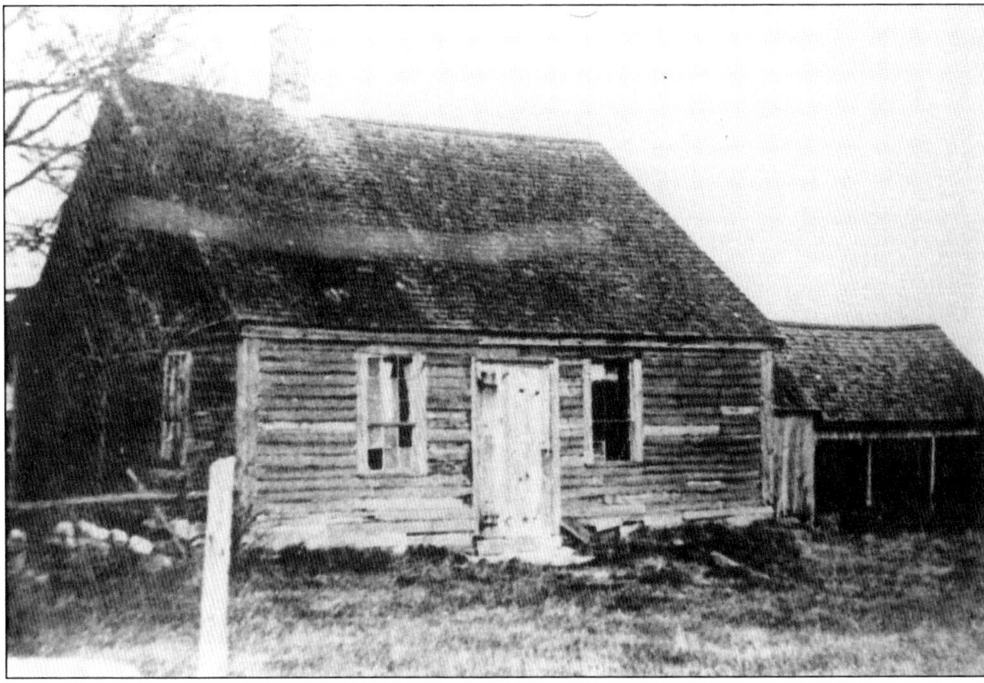

This photograph shows the Dennis Bowen home on Bear Hill.

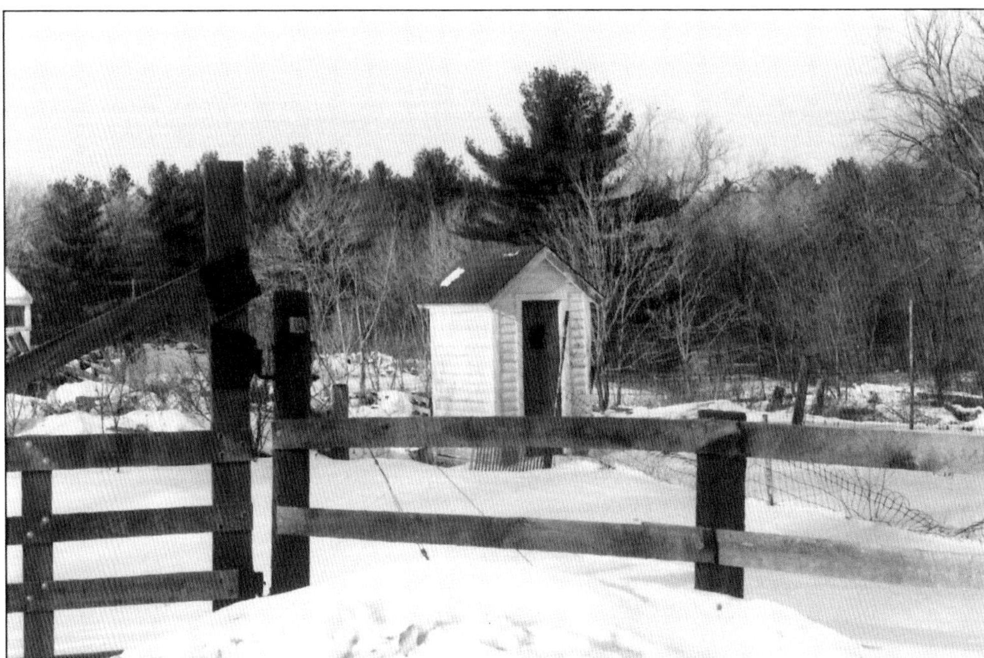

The outhouse at the Nathaniel "God" Smith home is now owned by Weston Nurseries.

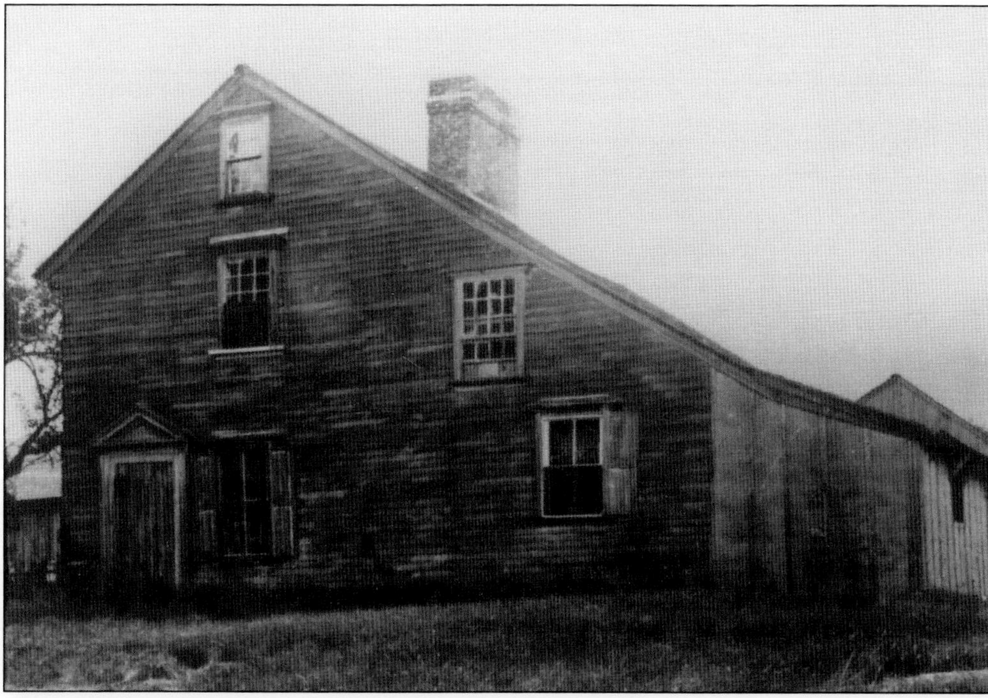

This view shows the side of the Nathaniel "God" Smith home on East Main Street.

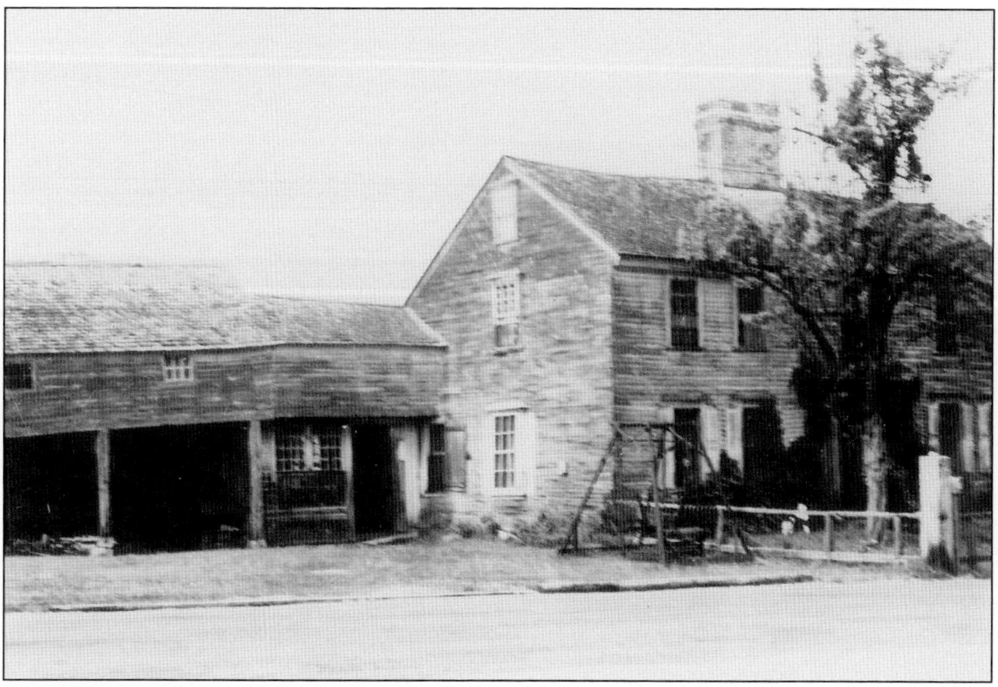

Another image shows the Nathaniel "God" Smith home on East Main Street—this time from the front.

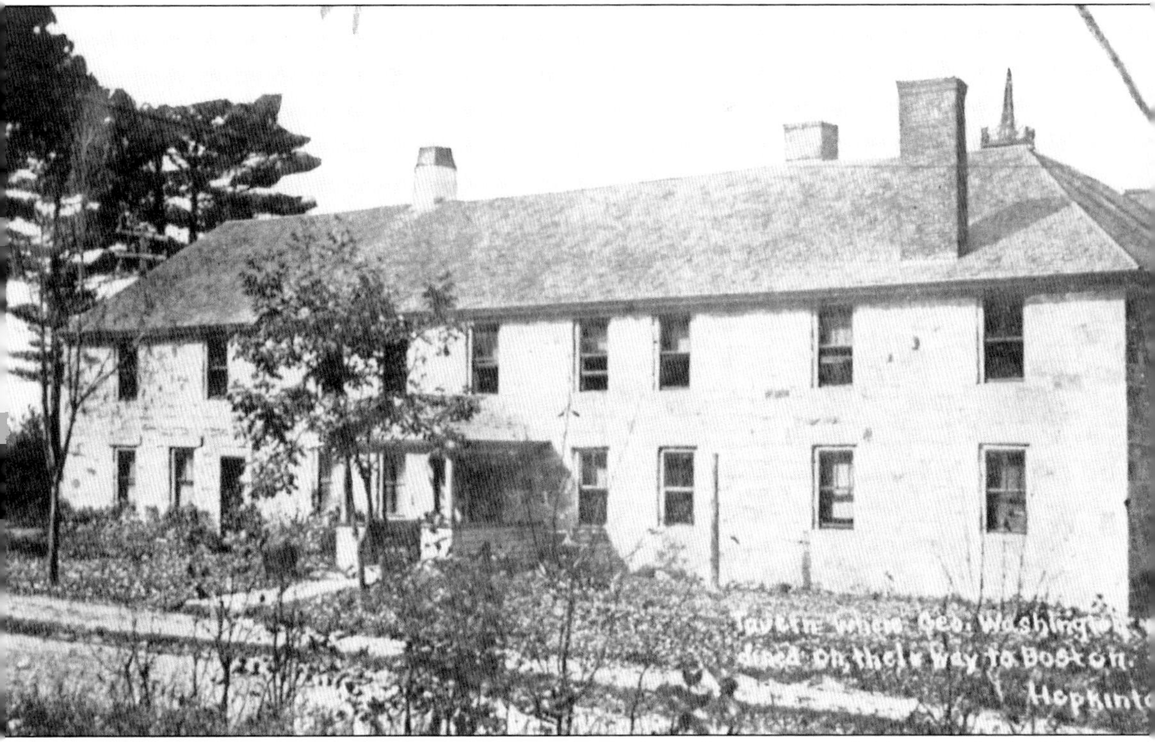

A tavern on East Main Street was located near the First Congregational Church. The building has been renovated and now includes several apartments.

Seven

Bear Hill

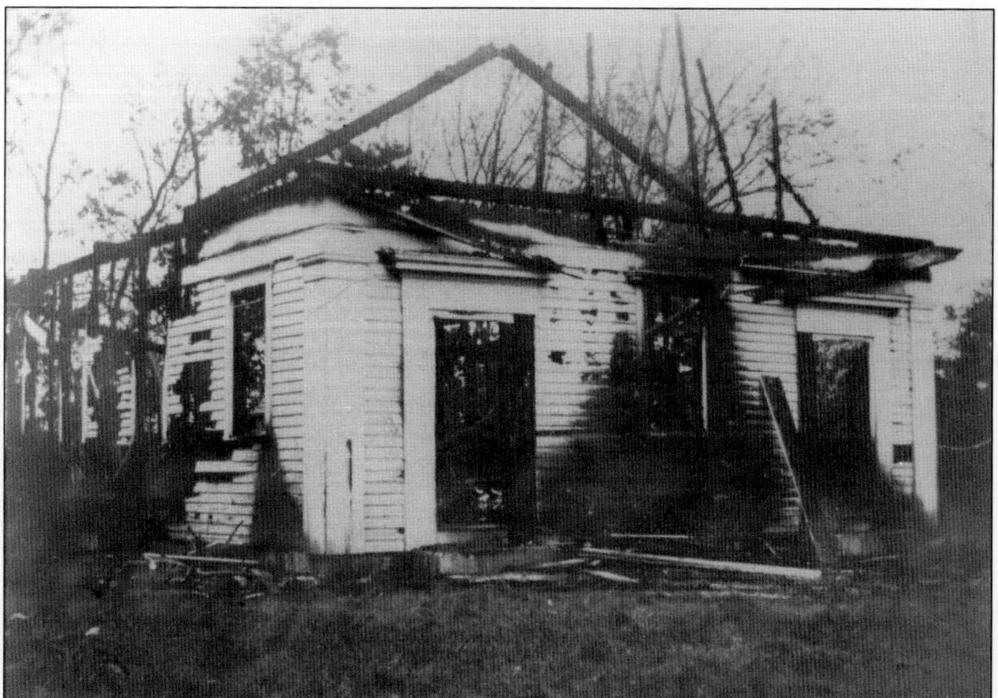

The Bear Hill School was a one-room district schoolhouse. This image, taken in 1930, shows the burned-out structure.

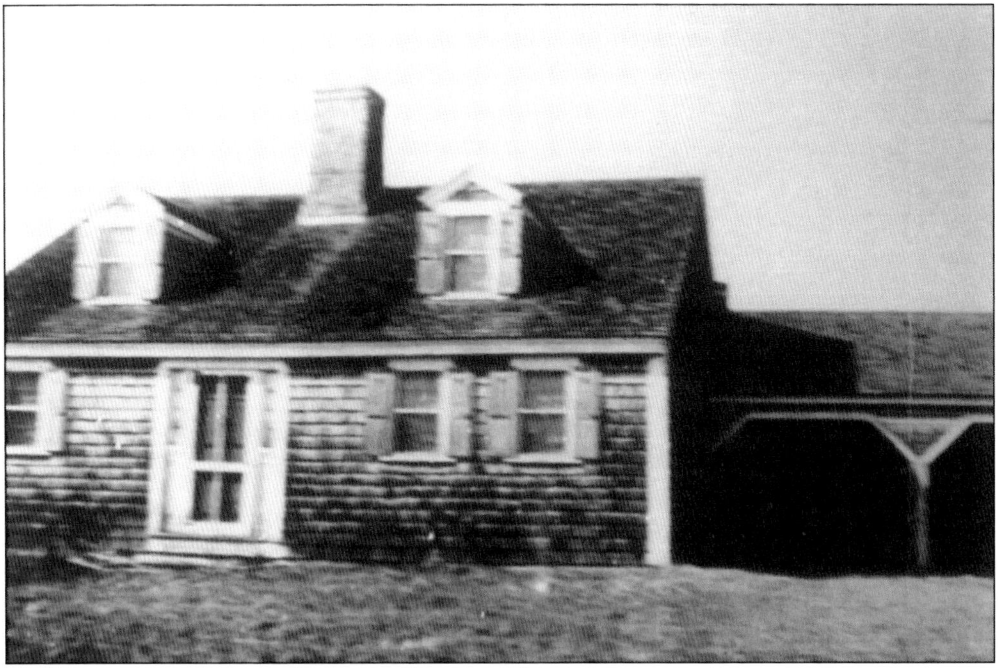

This old unidentified house shown in the 1800s was located on Bear Hill.

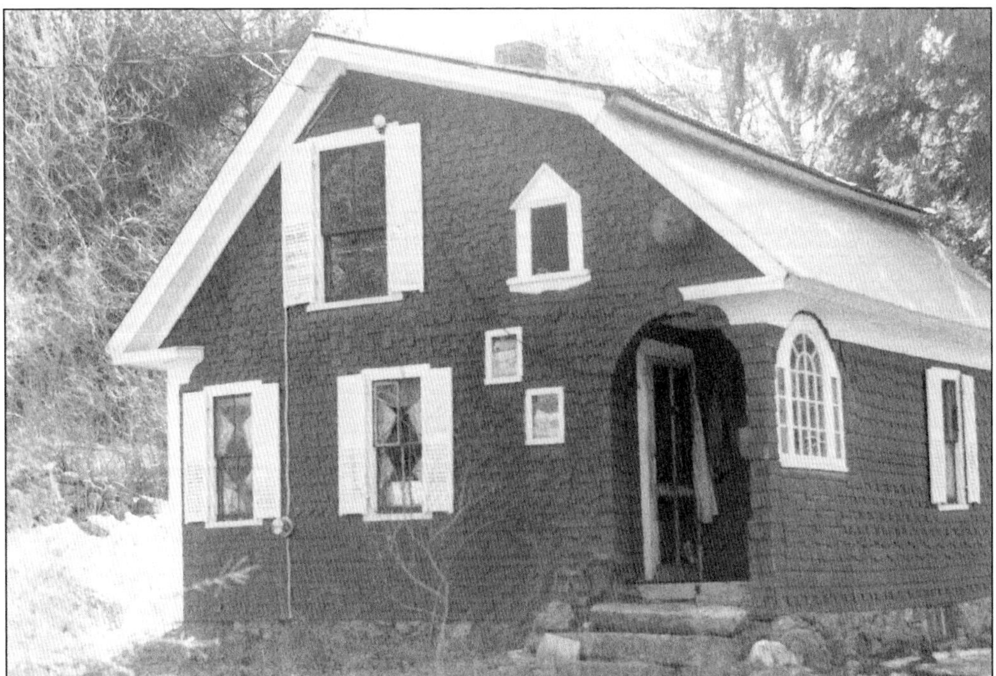

Harry Cheney was a horticulturist, a historian, and a collector of Indian artifacts. This was his home on School Street.

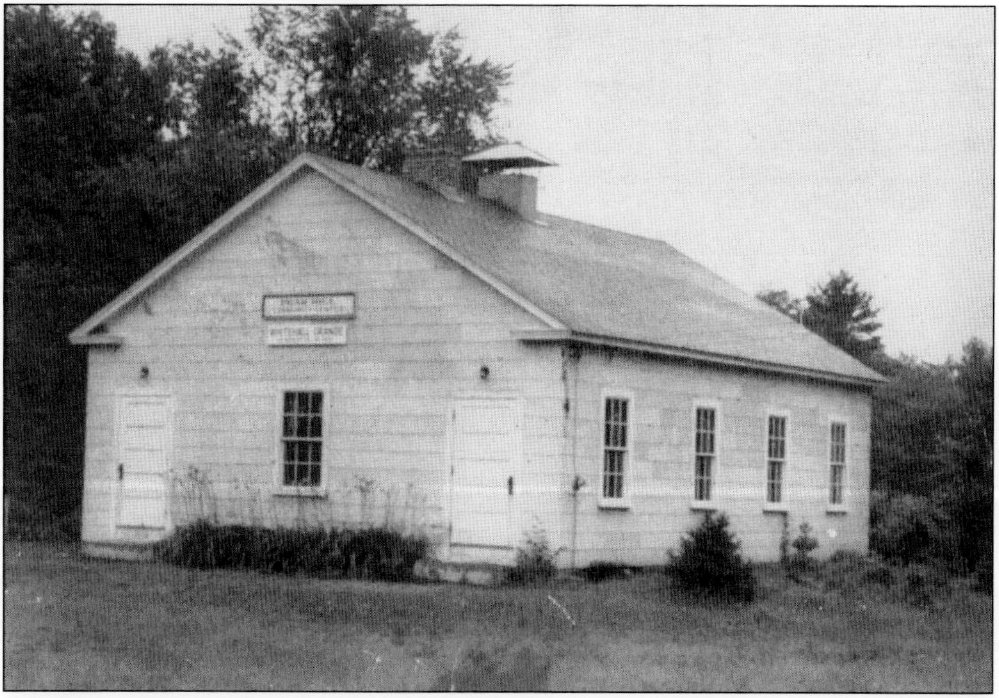

The Bear Hill Community Center and Whitehall Grange were used by residents of Bear Hill in 1930.

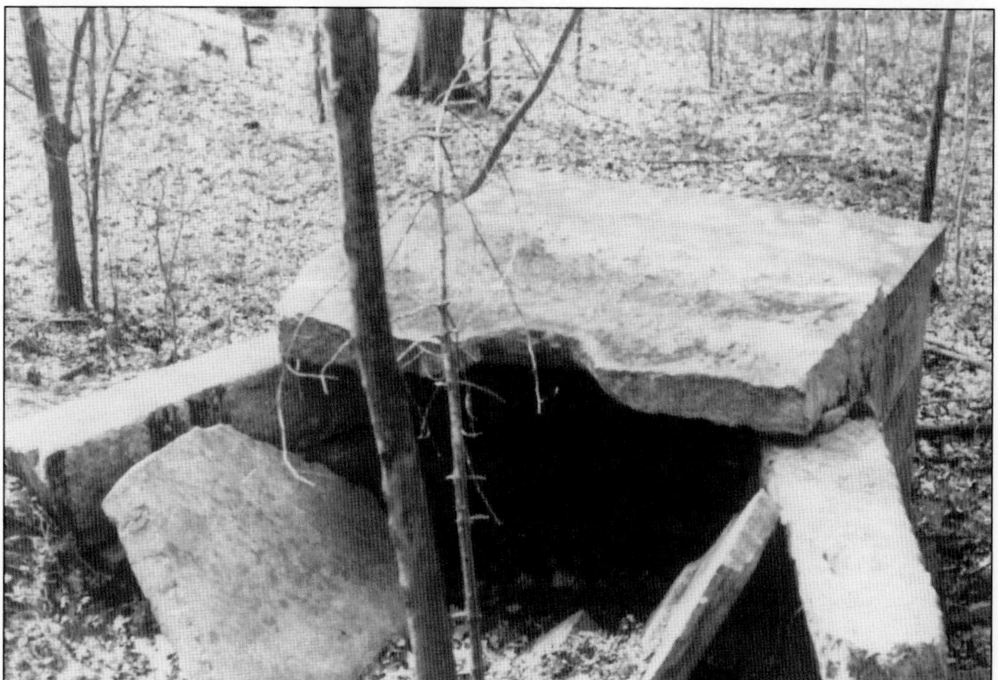

This mineral spring, one of many in the area, was located off Spring Street at Lake Whitehall.

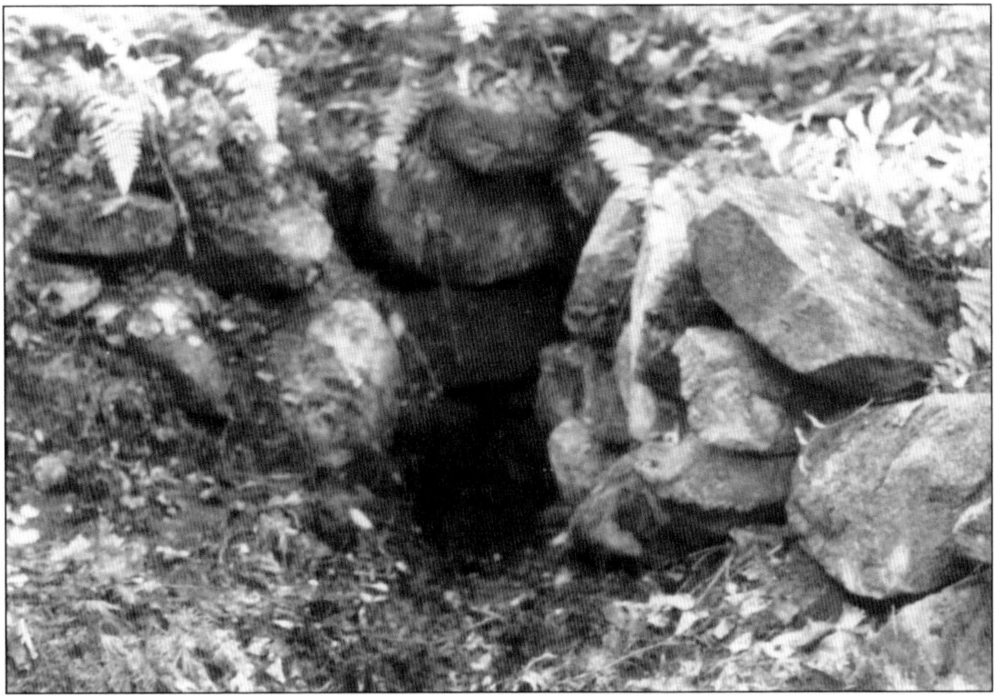

This sulphur mineral spring, located off Spring Street, was one of three springs.

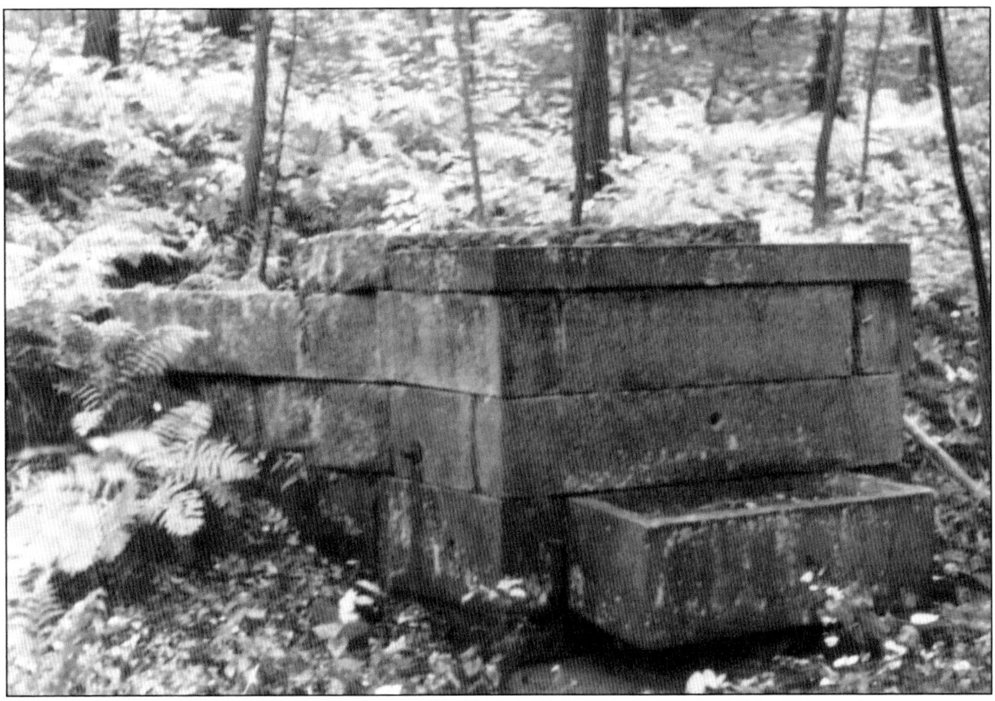

This magnesium mineral spring, located off Spring Street, was another natural resource in Bear Hill.

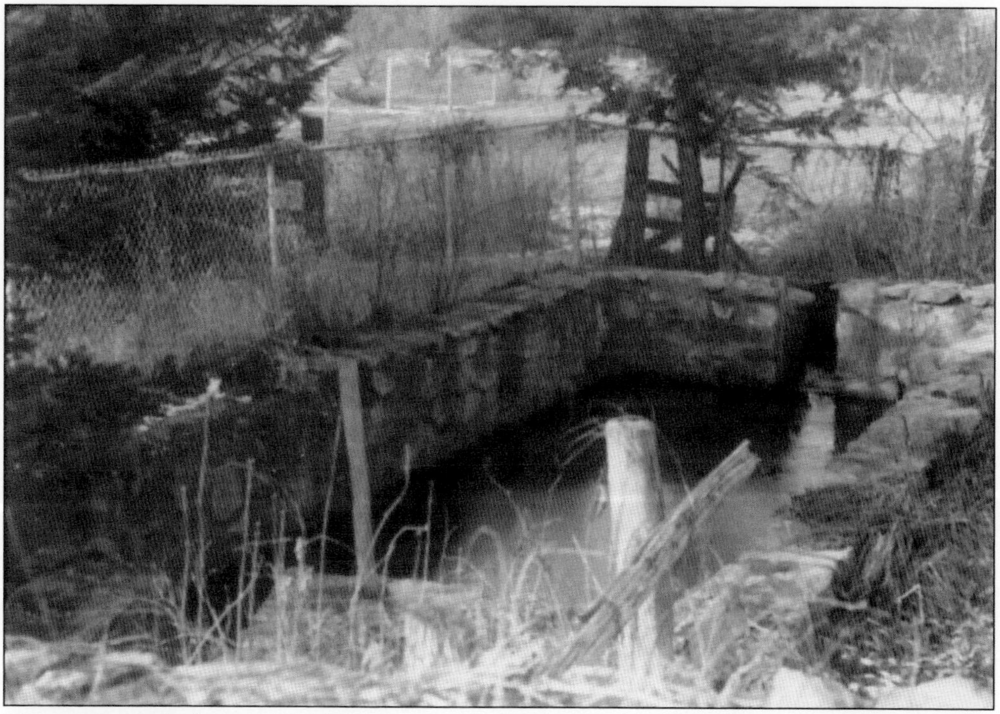

The granite-walled reservoir at a farm on Pond Street was owned by J. Howard Leman in 1940.

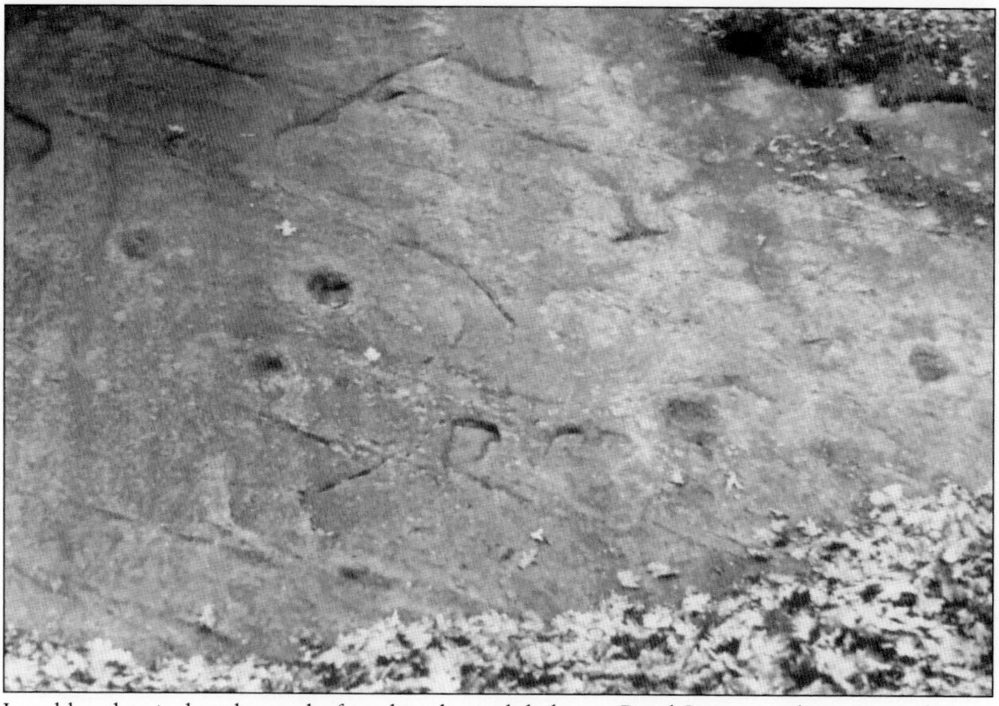

Local lore has it that the tracks found in the rock ledge on Pond Street are dinosaur tracks.

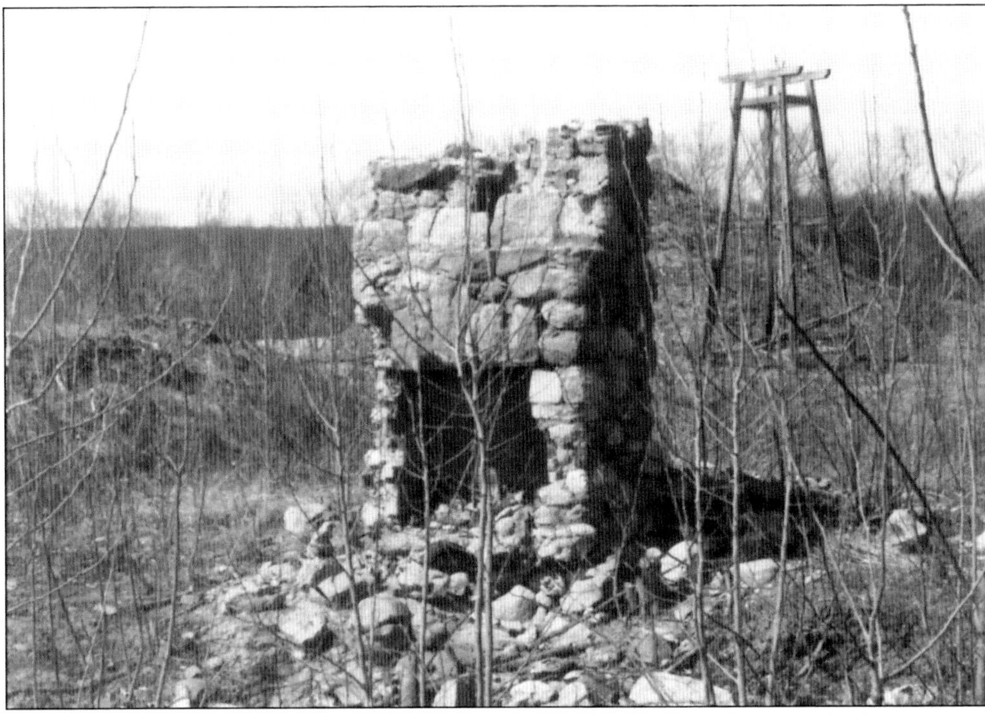

The base of a wooden water tank and the remnants of a fireplace are shown at the former site of a cottage located off Pond Street near Lake Whitehall.

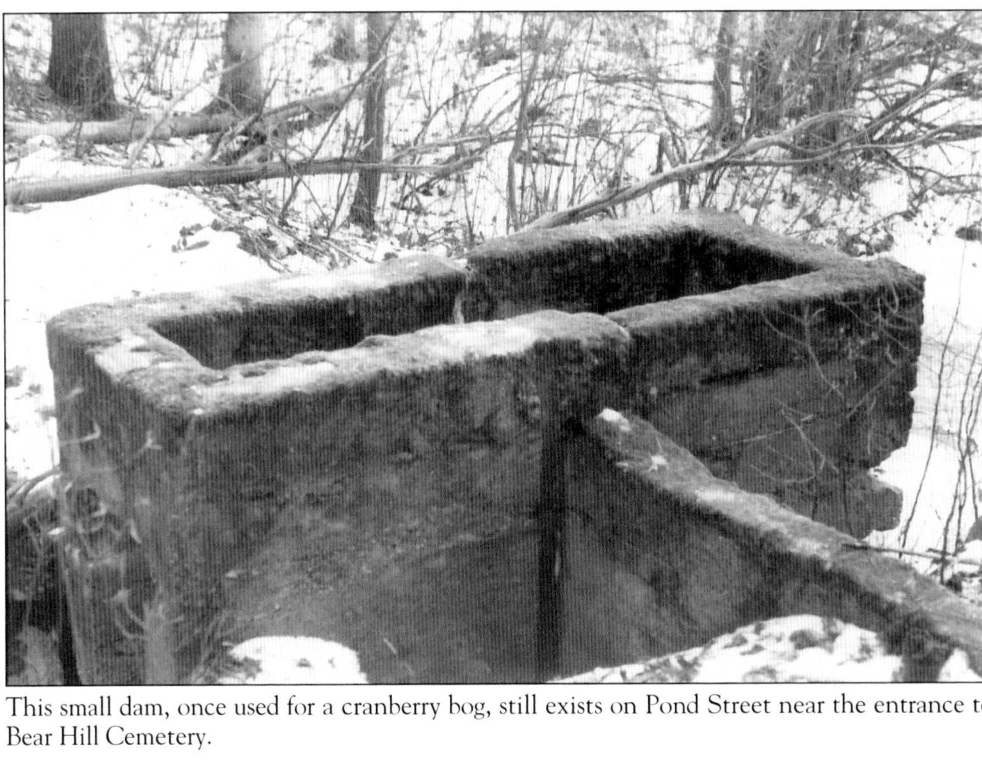

This small dam, once used for a cranberry bog, still exists on Pond Street near the entrance to Bear Hill Cemetery.

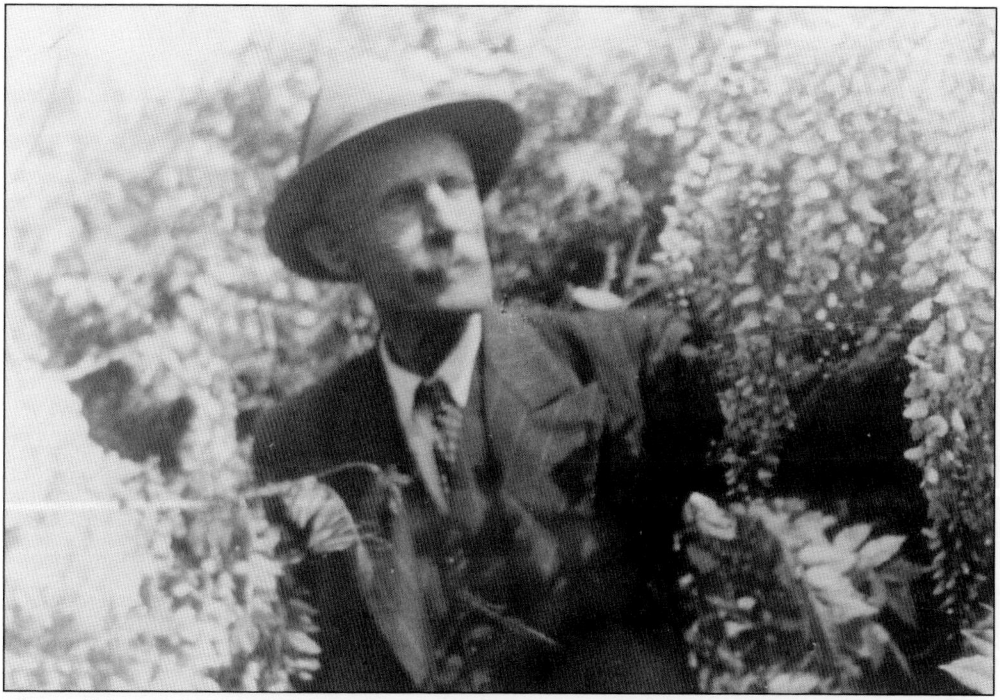

The well-known Harry Cheney was photographed surrounded by wisteria blossoms on School Street in 1940.

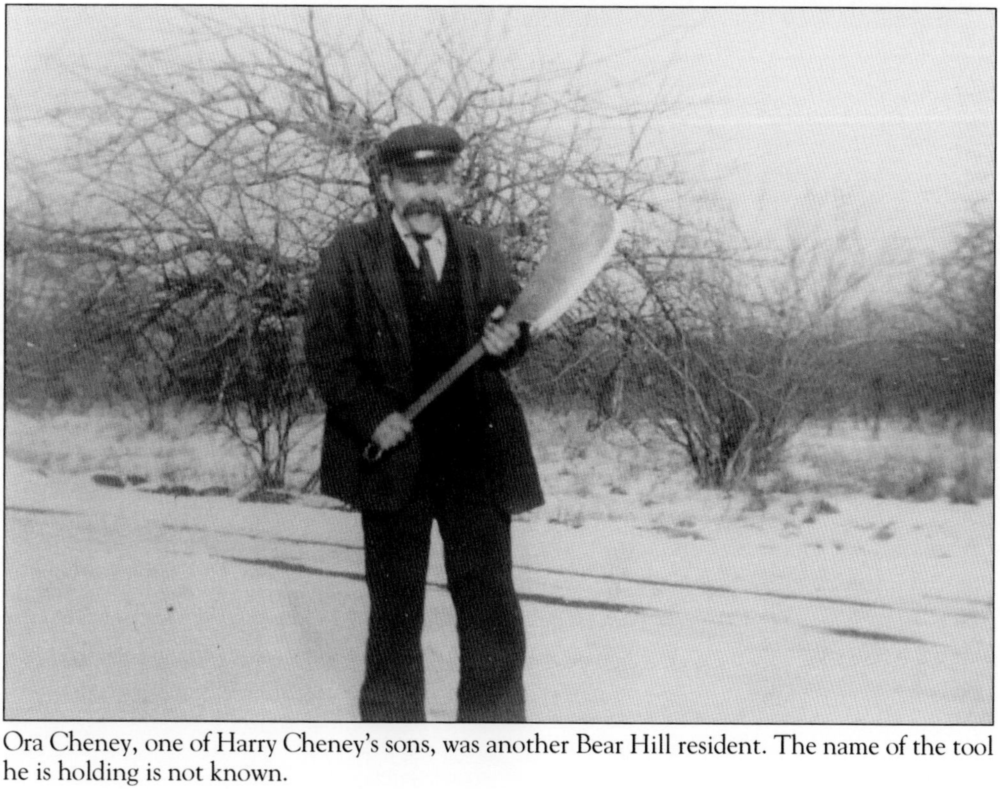

Ora Cheney, one of Harry Cheney's sons, was another Bear Hill resident. The name of the tool he is holding is not known.

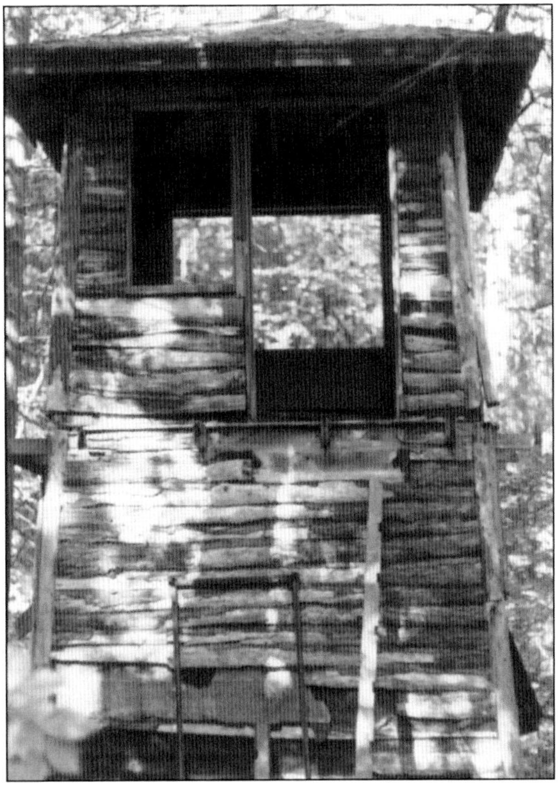

This well house and observation tower were located off Pond Street and used by cottagers near Lake Whitehall during the 1930s.

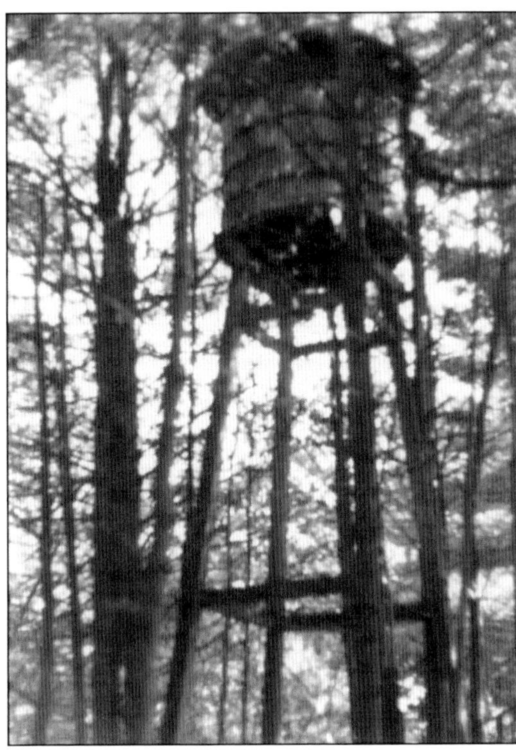

This wooden water tank was located off Pond Street near Lake Whitehall in 1930.

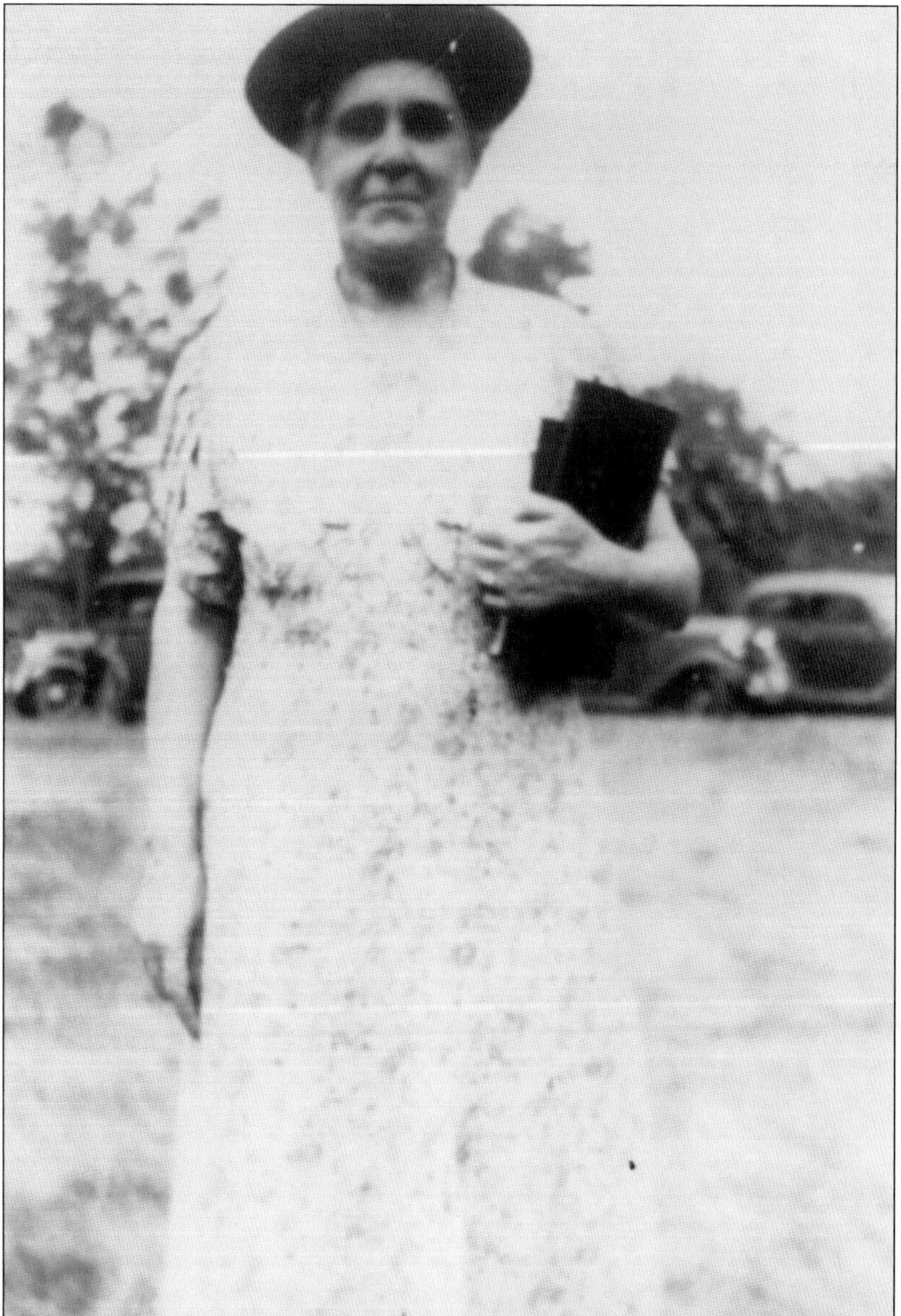

Carrie Madden was the last teacher at the Bear Hill School. She taught students here from 1909 to 1933.

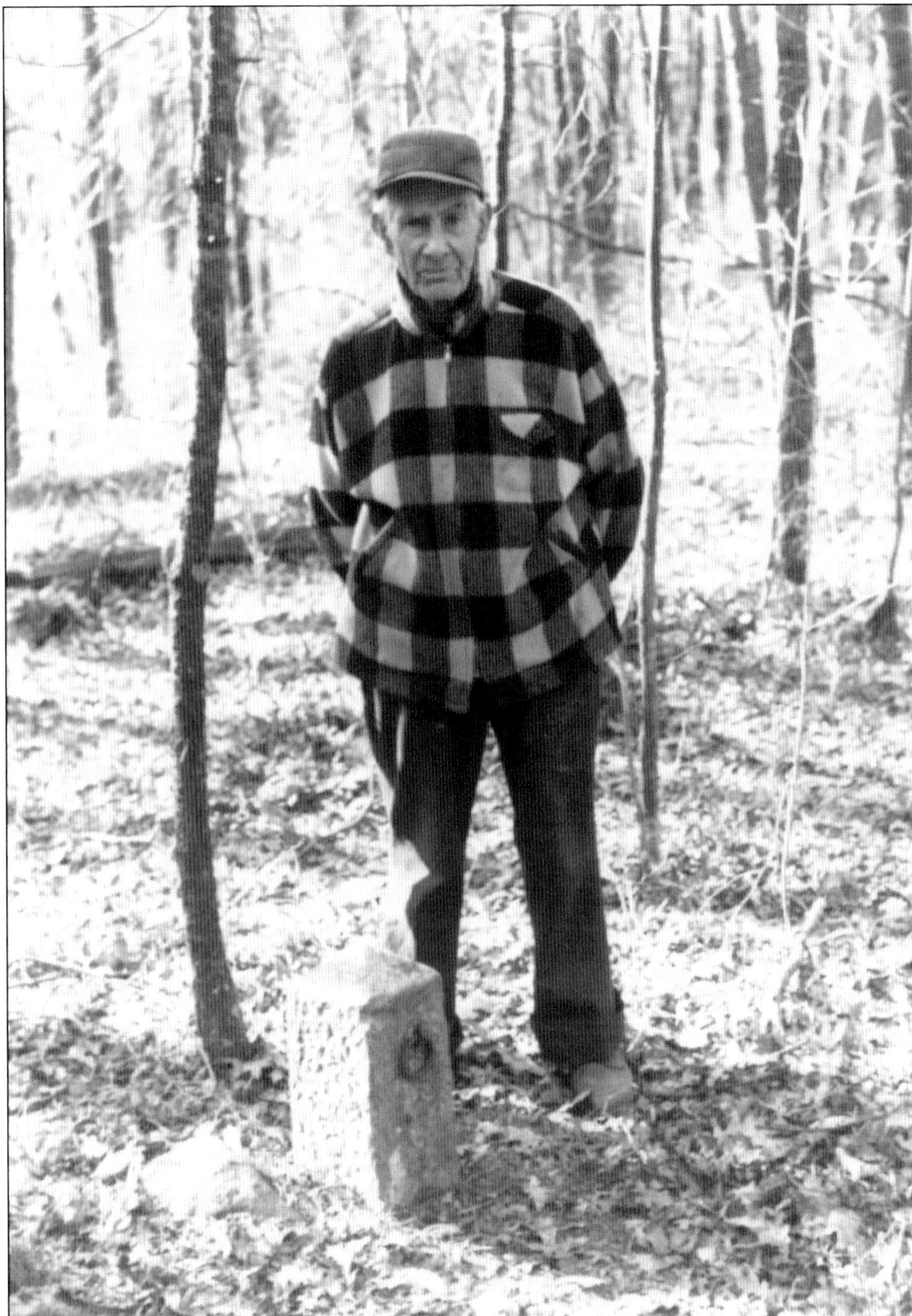

Harry Babbitt, pictured here in 1980, was a longtime Bear Hill resident and made his home in a converted school bus. He was a farmer, and he owned a beautiful pair of work horses.

Eight

Fires and Firefighters

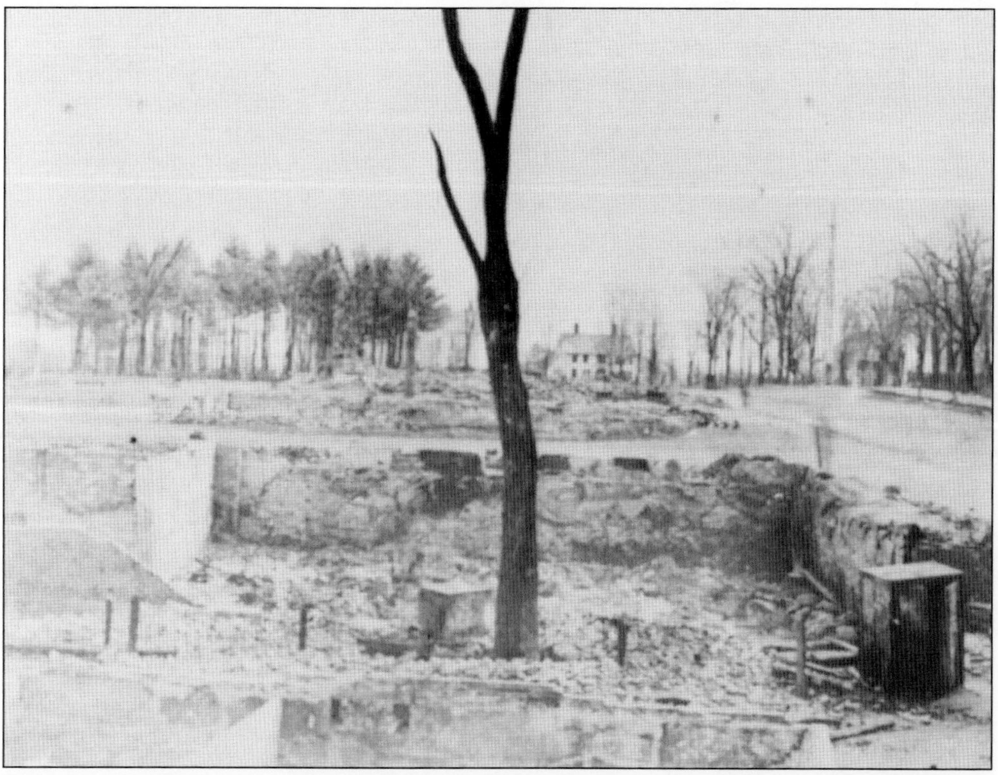

This section of Main Street shows the devastation caused by a large fire in 1876. A larger fire occurred in 1882, and a third major fire (in 1900) caused Hopkinton's strong presence in the shoe and boot industry to be completely and permanently lost.

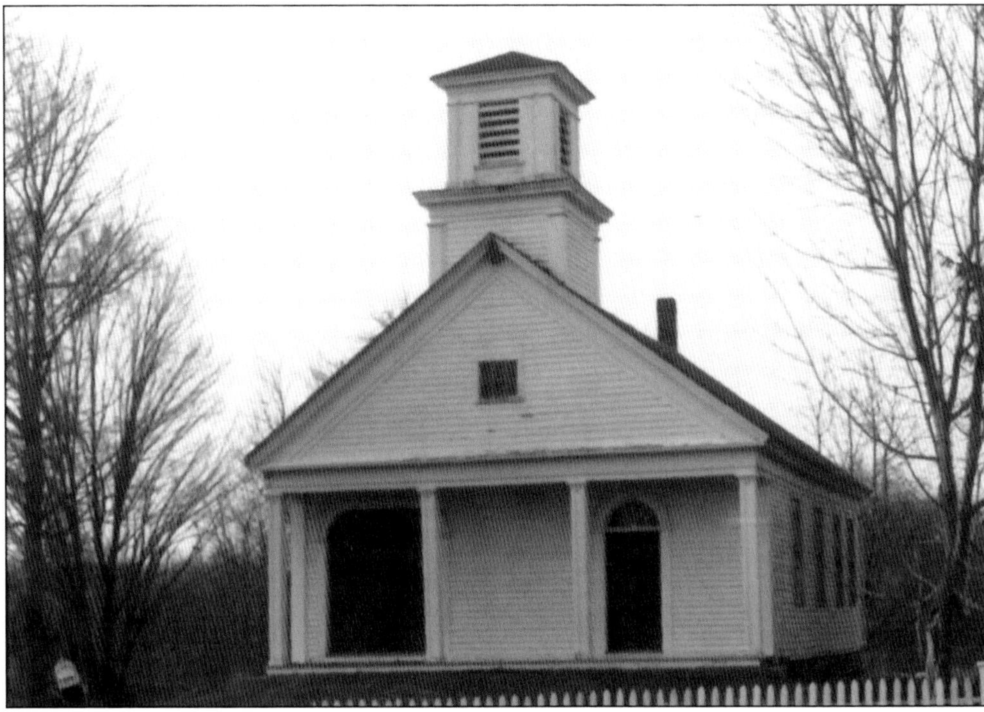

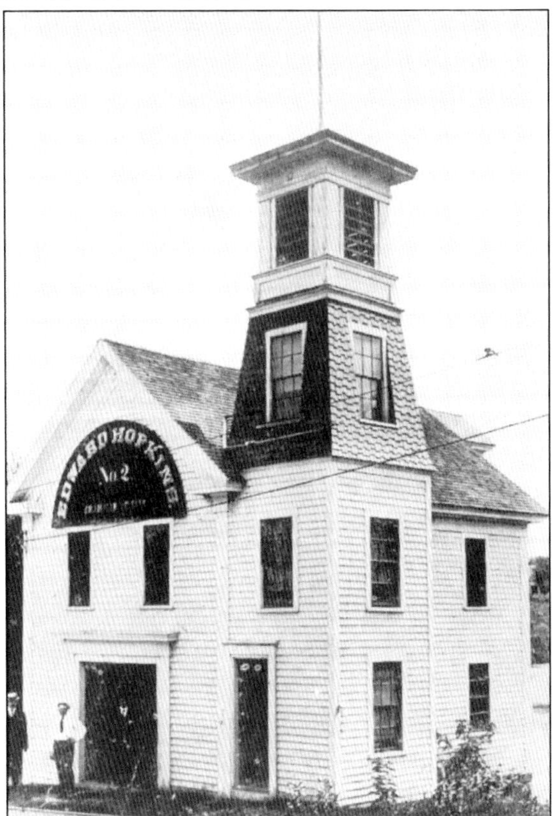

The former No. 3 engine house was located at Hayden Rowe. It was built in 1816 as a Methodist church. Hand tubs were stored inside the gable end about 1854. The building was once owned by sports promoter George Brown, and dances were held in the old engine house during the 1920s and 1930s.

The original engine house is shown at Woodville in 1909. It was purchased by Clarence Farrar in 1980s.

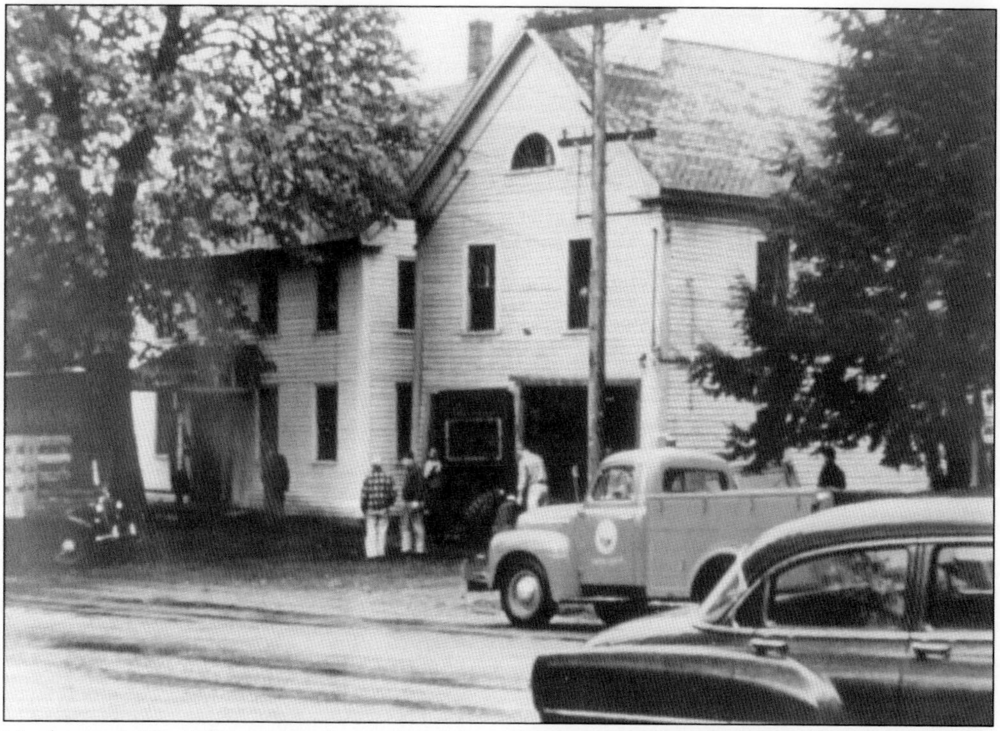

Hopkinton's No. 1 fire station, located on Main Street, was replaced in 1954. The nearby house was owned by Joseph and Nellie Ambroge.

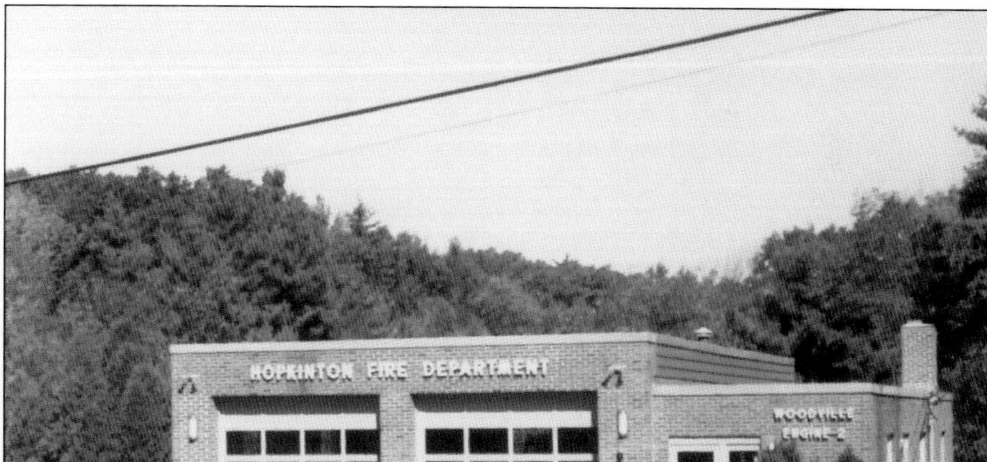

The new fire station at Woodville replaced the old engine house. The new facility is shown here in this 1980 photograph.

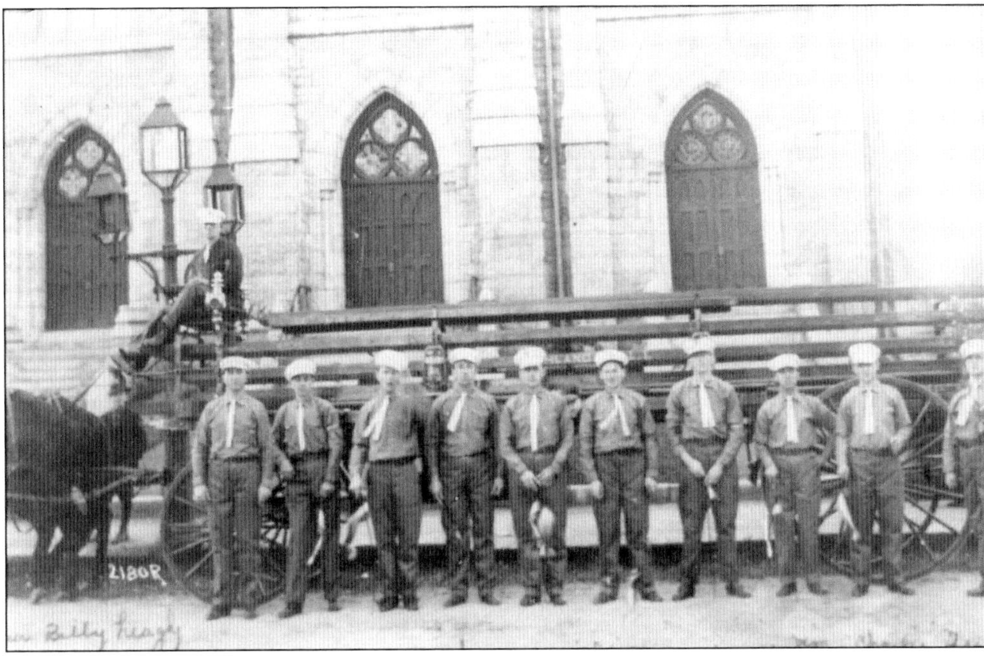

Highland Hook and Ladder No. 1's horse-drawn ladder truck was photographed in 1911. The driver is Billy Leaghy. From left to right are Joe McGowan, Jack McManus, Jack McCauliffe, Jim Long, unidentified, Jim Foley, Charlie Hollien, Frank Coffy, Mike Ward, and Capt. Henry Pyne.

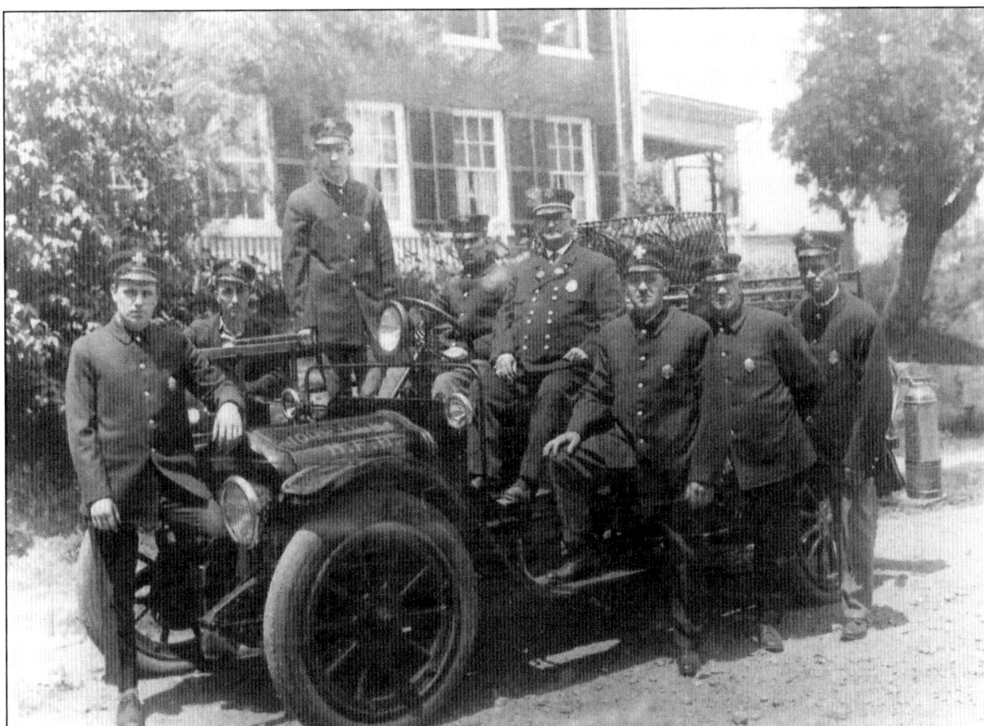

Fire department personnel posed for this picture at Woodville station, probably in the 1920s.

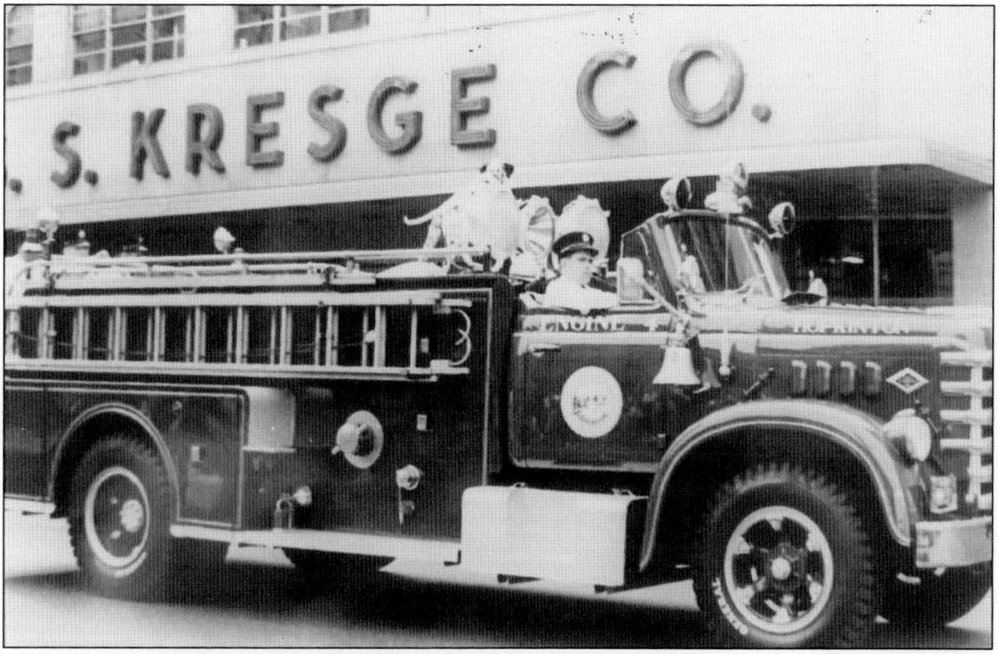

Engine 4 was a 1955 Diamond T. This picture was taken during a parade in Worcester. The driver was Richard Bartlett, Paul Keaney was the passenger, and the dog's name was Diesel.

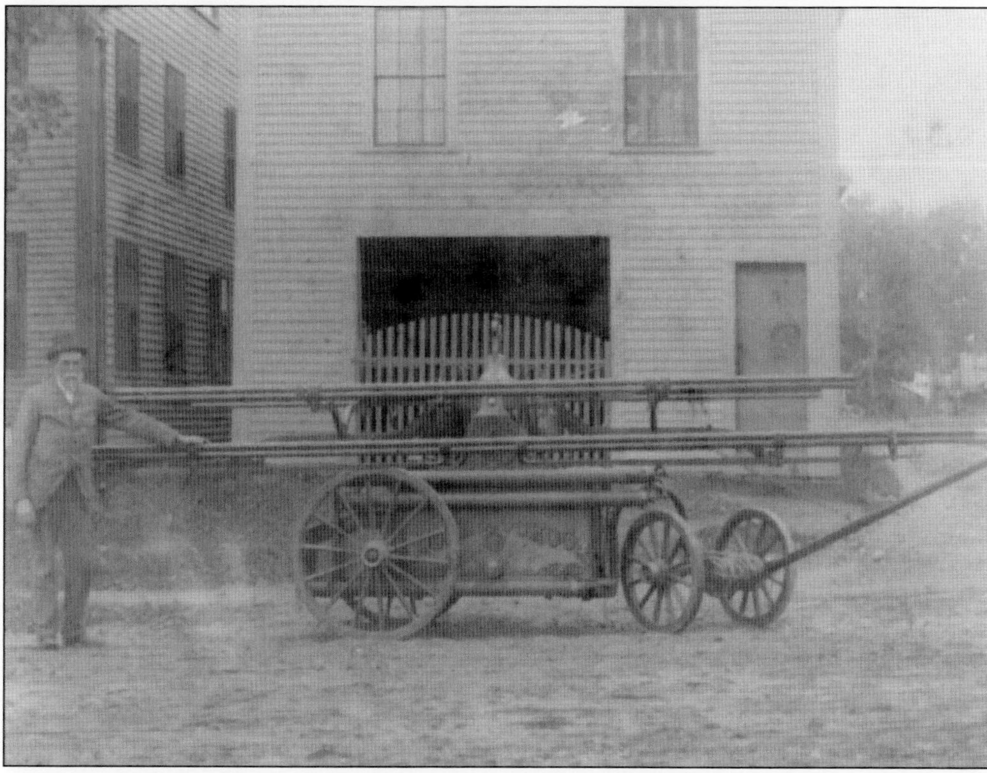

"Quinsigamog" was the name of a hand pumper based at Woodville for many years. It became a champion pumper at firemen's musters.

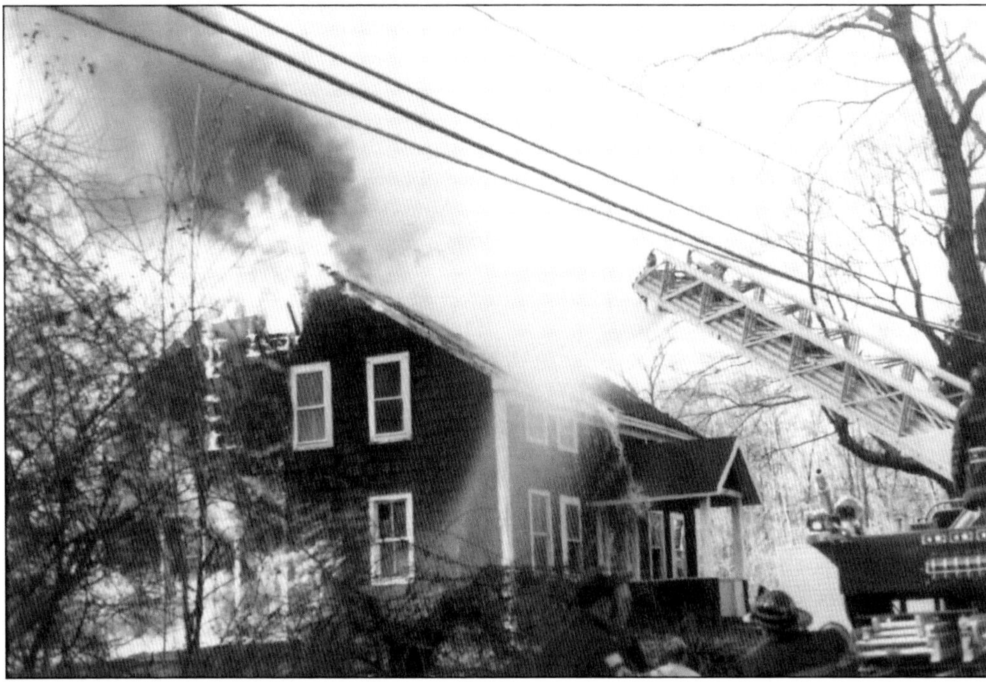

The fire department burned the former Zani home on Ash Street as part of its training program on November 13, 1983. The aerial ladder truck belonged to the Holliston Fire Department.

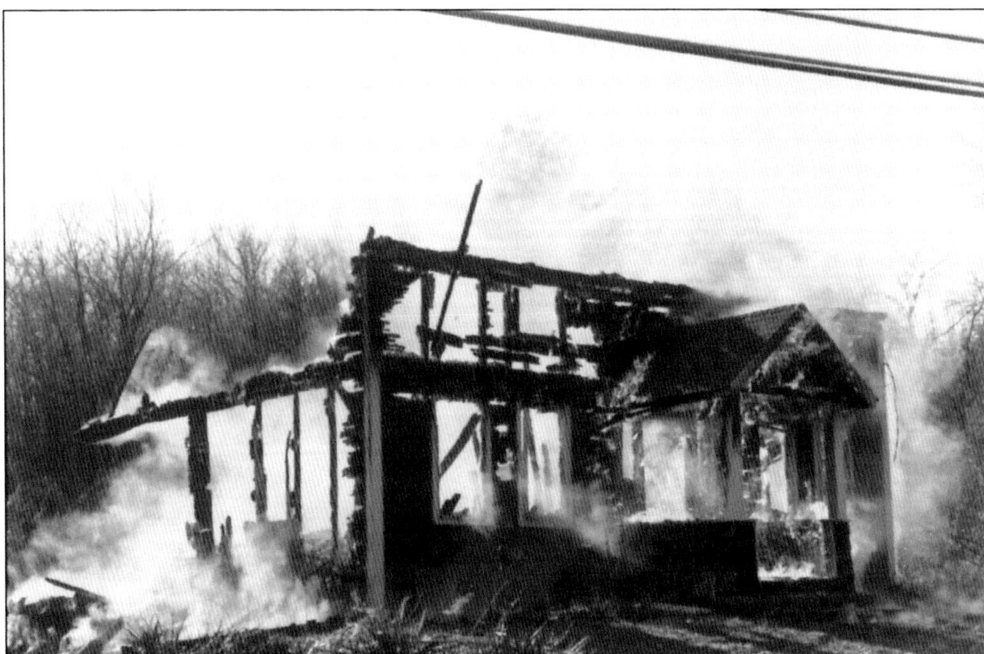

This is a front view of the Zani house fire during the fire department's training exercise on November 13, 1983.

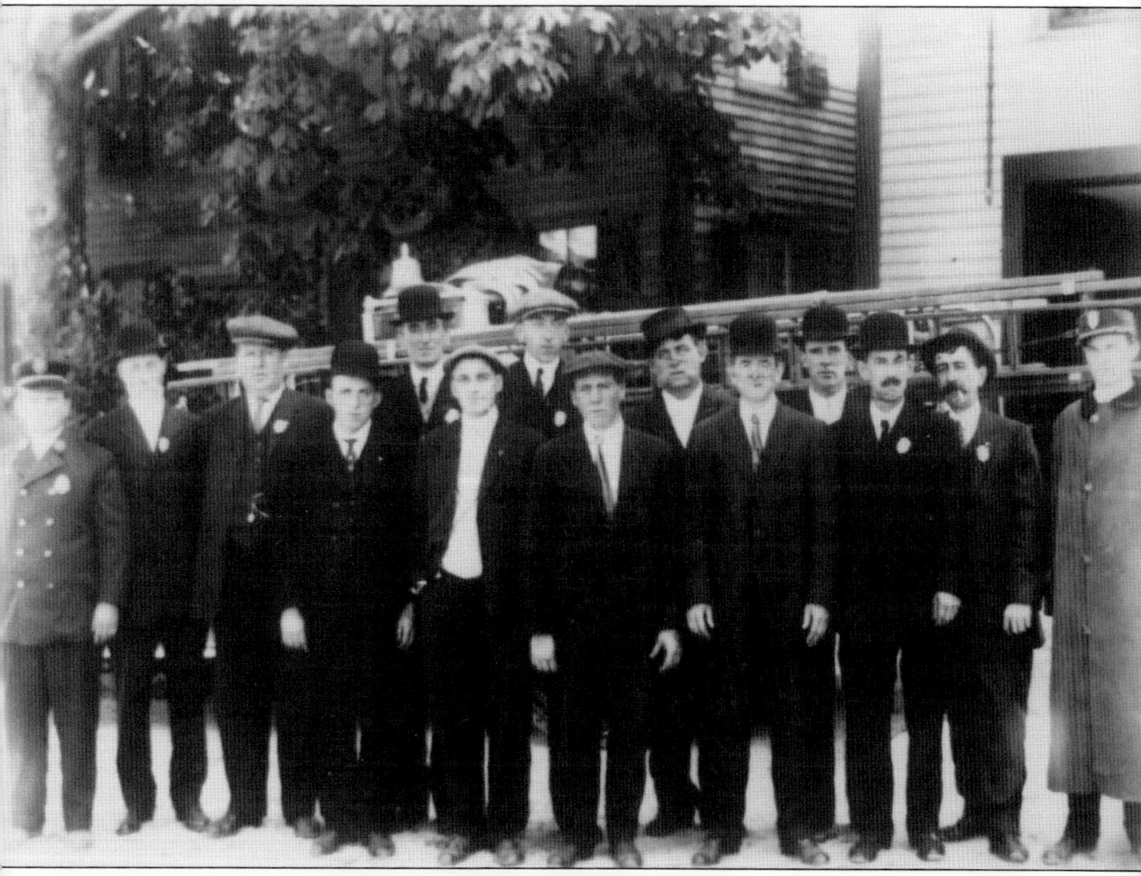

According to the back of the photograph, pictured are, from left to right: (front row) Chief Tim Danahy, J.D. Stewart, Tom Burke, Gerry O'Brien, Charles Marshall, Jim Lenane, William Monahan, Waldo Smith, Perley Etta, and Alex Macmillan; (back row) Mattie Conlon (police chief), Tony Cosgrove, and Eddie Buck.

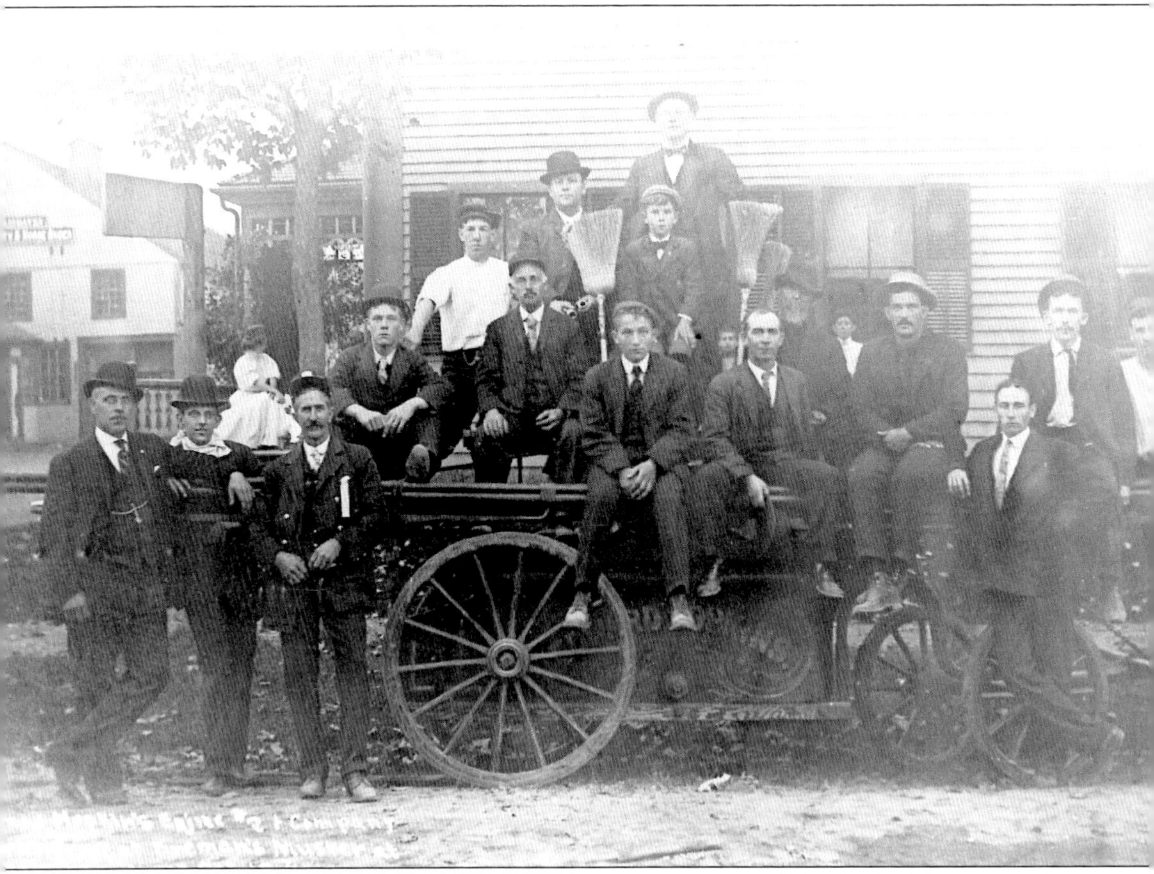

This image shows the Edward Hopkins Engine No. 2 station at Woodville. The men had just won first prize at a firemen's muster on October 17, 1908.

Nine

Railroads and Trolleys

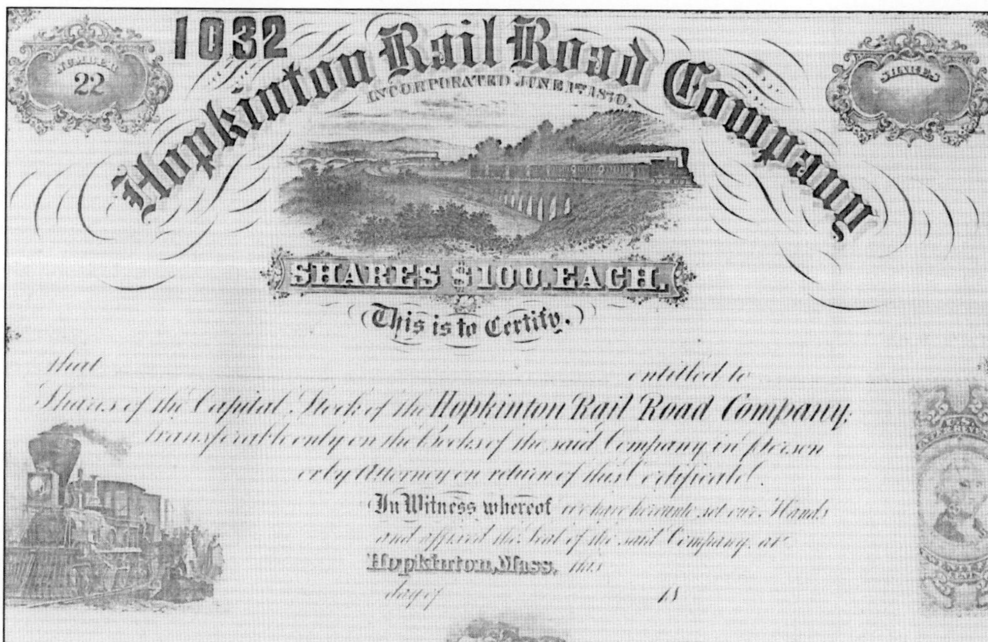

This is an 1890 Hopkinton Railroad Company stock certificate. Original certificates were made by the American Bank Note Co.

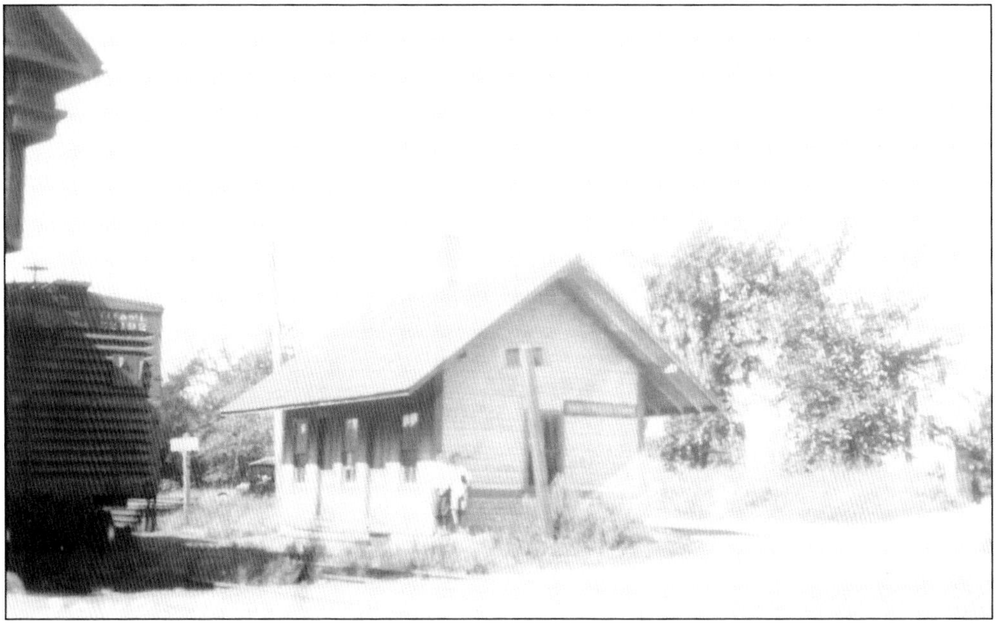

The New York, New Haven & Hartford railroad station, located on Main Street, is shown here in 1890.

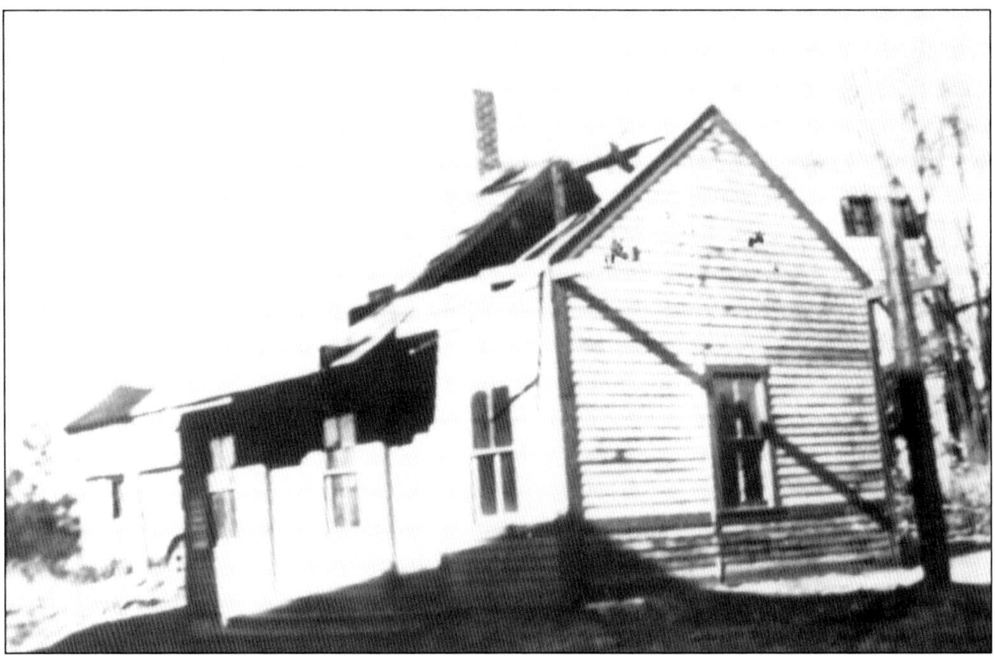

Hopkinton's New York, New Haven & Hartford railroad station appears here after part of its roof blew away during a windstorm in 1938.

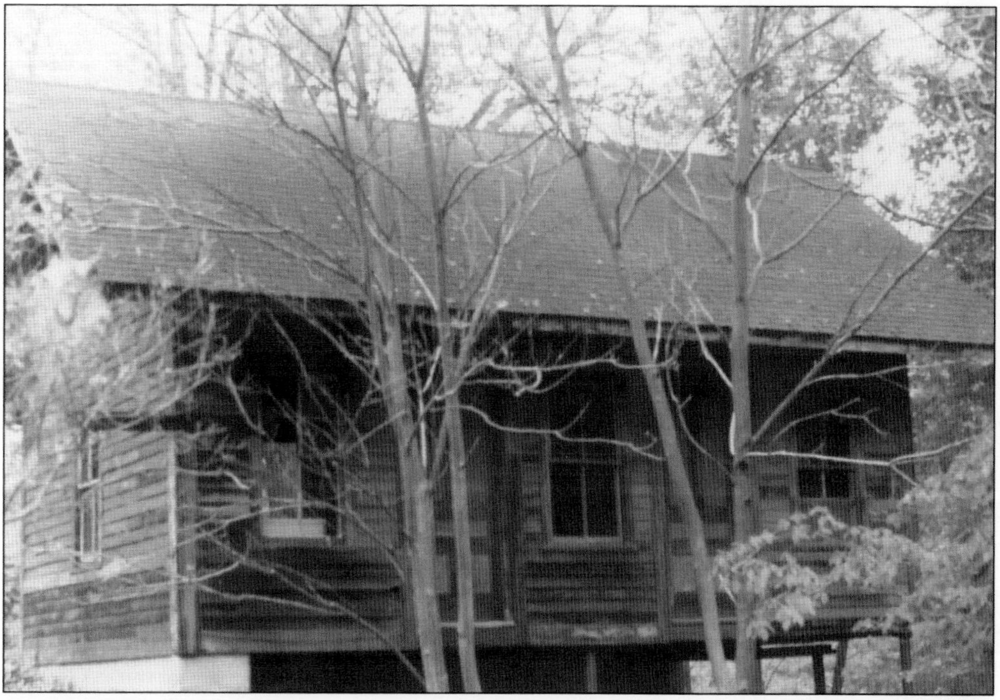

The Hopkinton railroad station was relocated to private property on Pond Street and is seen here in 1975.

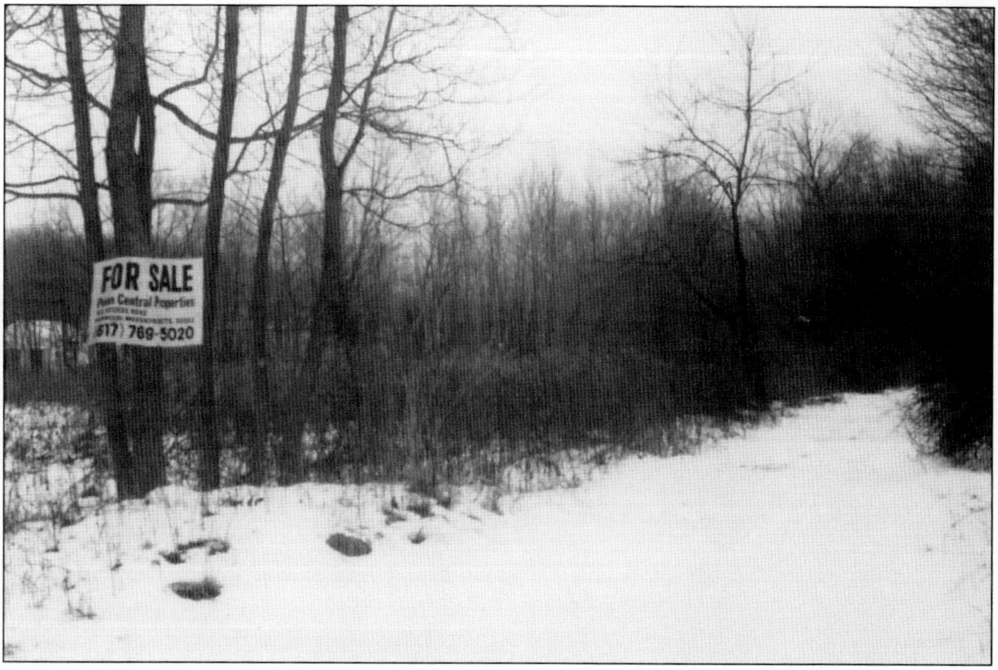

In this 1980 photograph, part of the New York, New Haven & Hartford Railroad roadbed is visible near the Granite Street crossing.

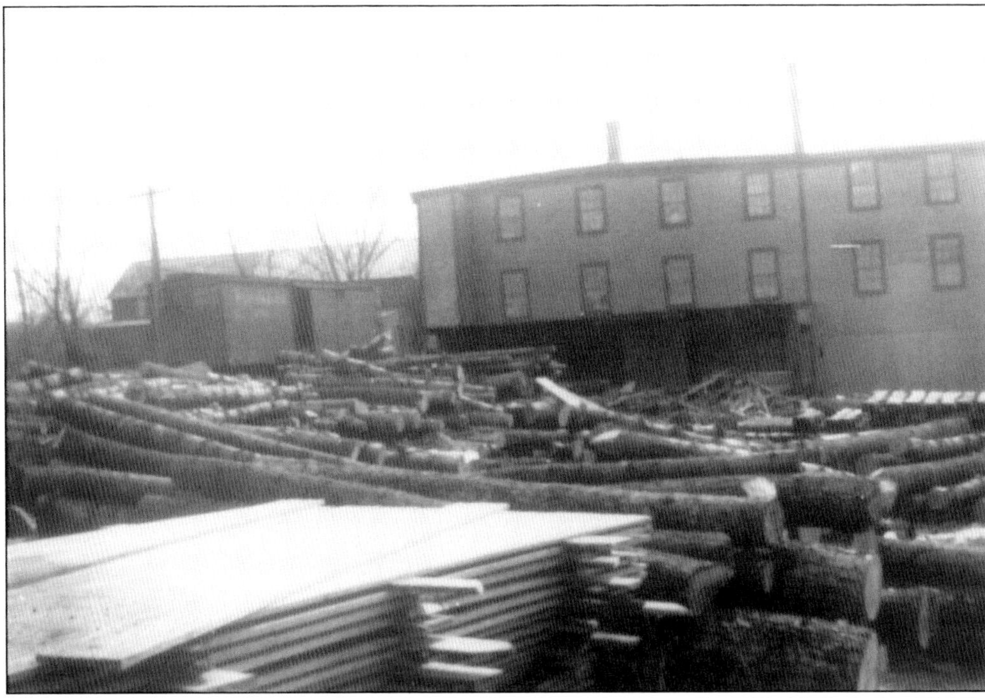

A railroad boxcar was photographed in 1904 off Meserve Street at the J.H. Claflin sawmill. The large building at the rear of the yard was the Crooks and Root boot and shoe shop.

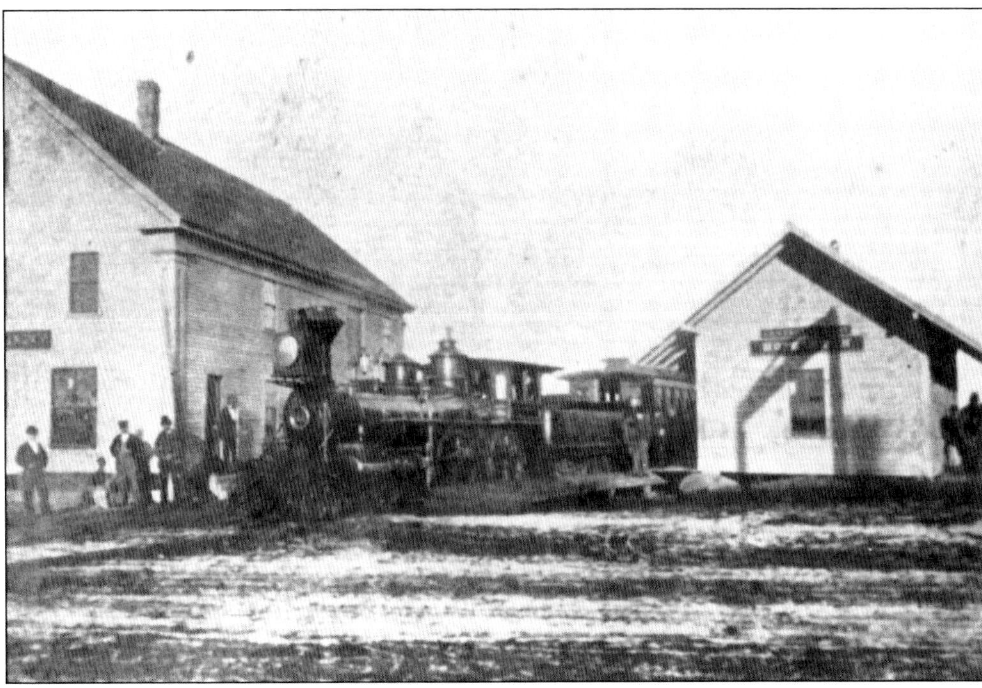

The Hopkinton Railroad passenger train, seen here in 1890, stopped at the Hopkinton railroad station on Main Street.

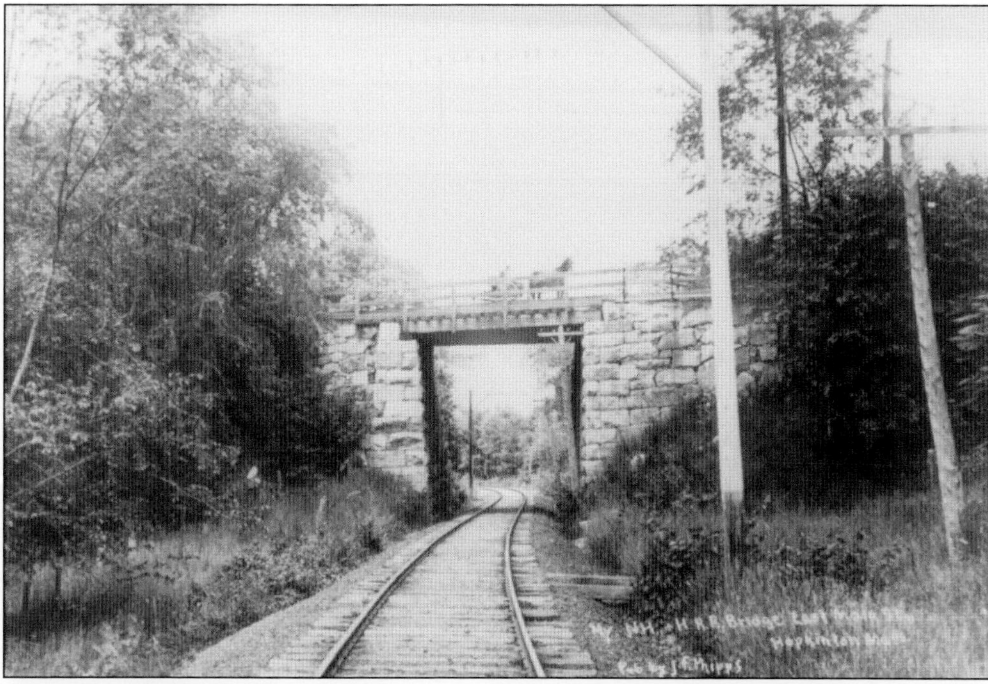

This railroad bridge was located on East Main Street. Note the telltale seen in the foreground in this 1930 image looking toward Ashland.

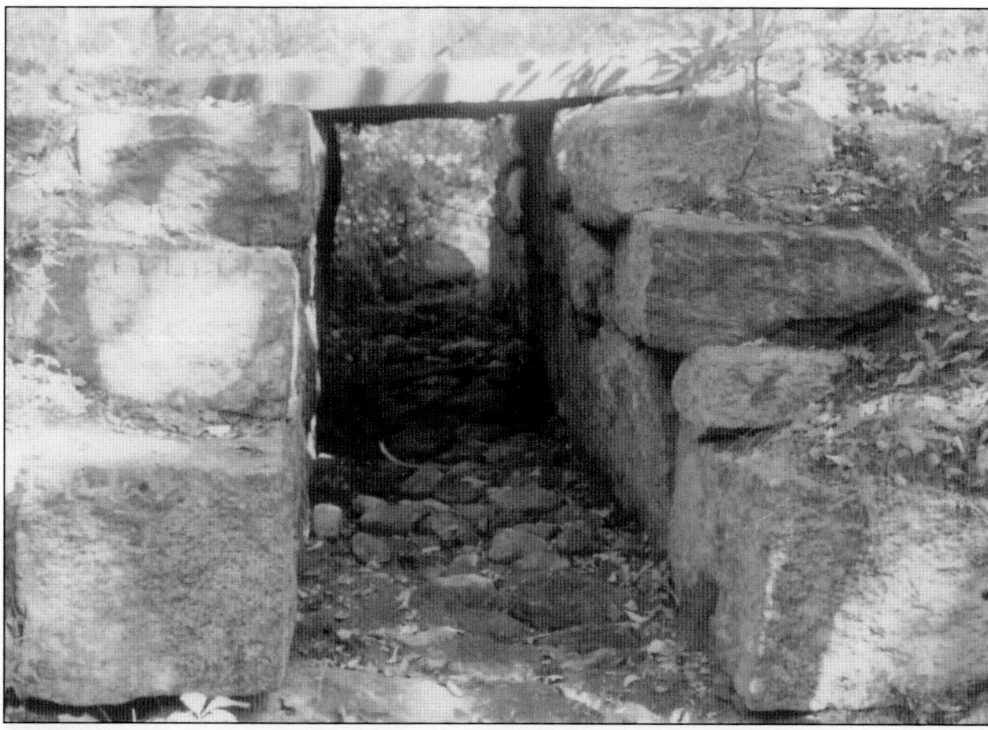

A granite block culvert was located between Chamberlain Street and Route 135, as shown in this 1978 image.

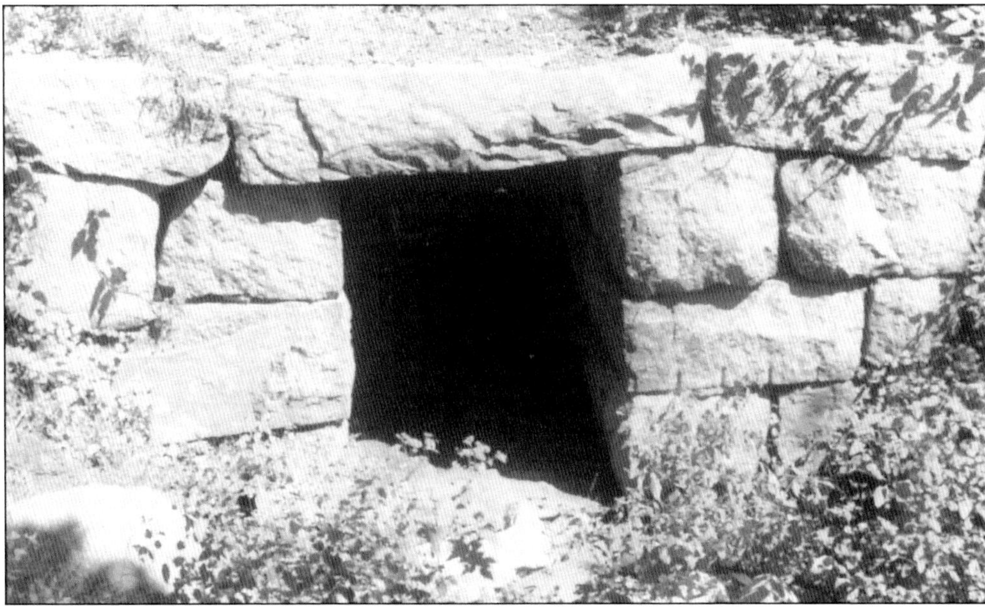

Another 1978 shot shows the the granite block culvert between Chamberlain Street and Route 135.

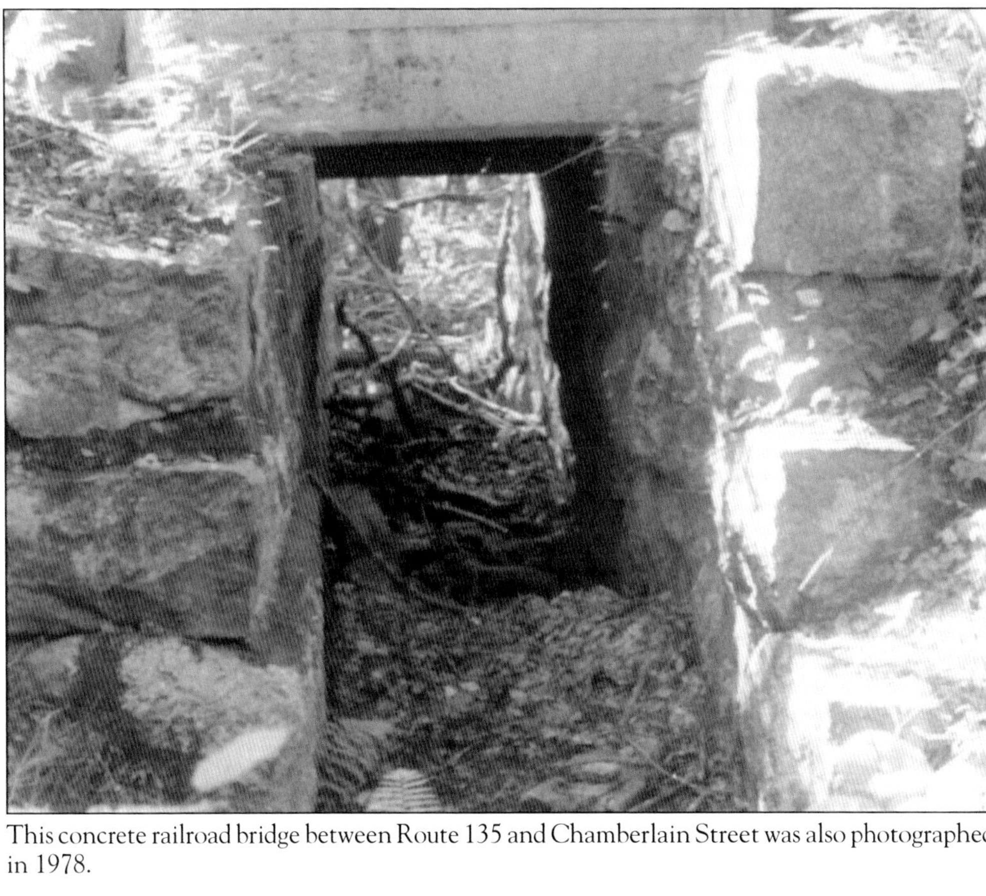

This concrete railroad bridge between Route 135 and Chamberlain Street was also photographed in 1978.

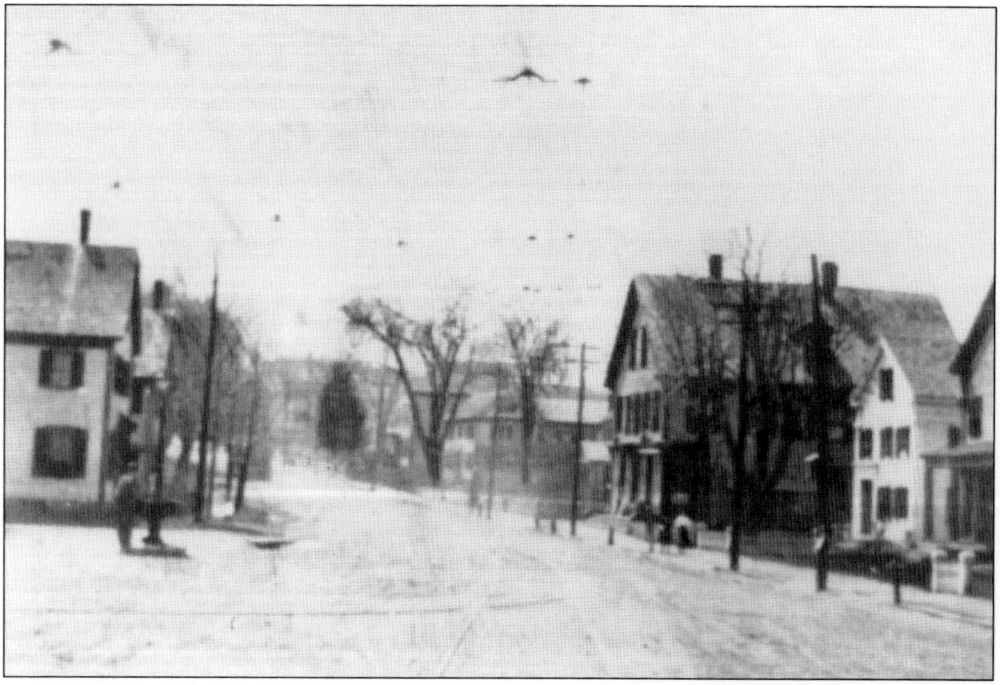

In this early turn-of-the-century photograph, looking west, one can see the trolley tracks on Main Street near the car barn.

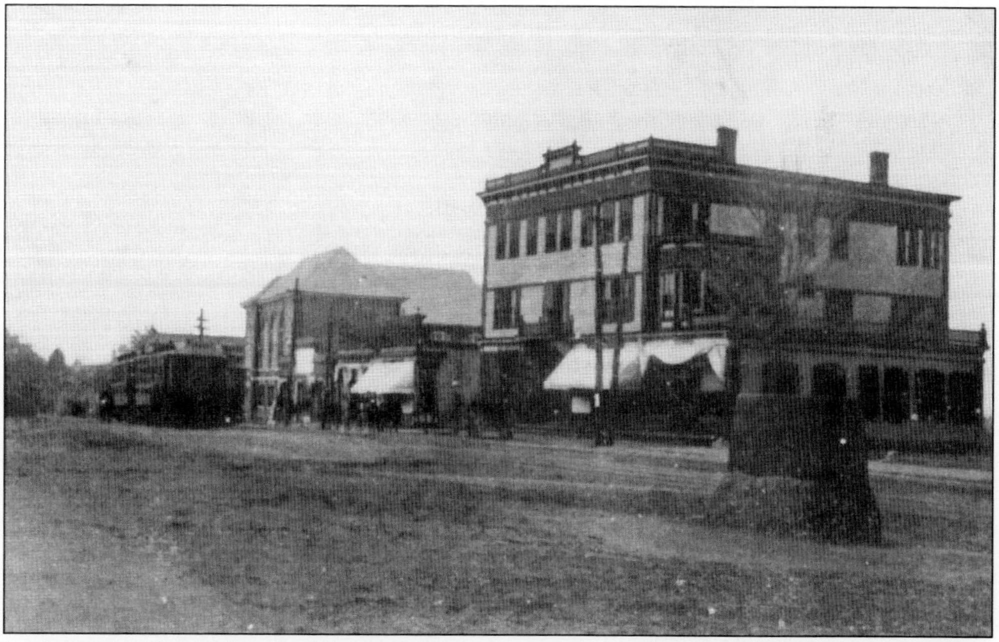

Looking west along Main Street in the 1910s, one sees two trolley cars. Note the town hall near the electric cars and the watering trough at the intersection of Main and Hayden Rowe Streets.

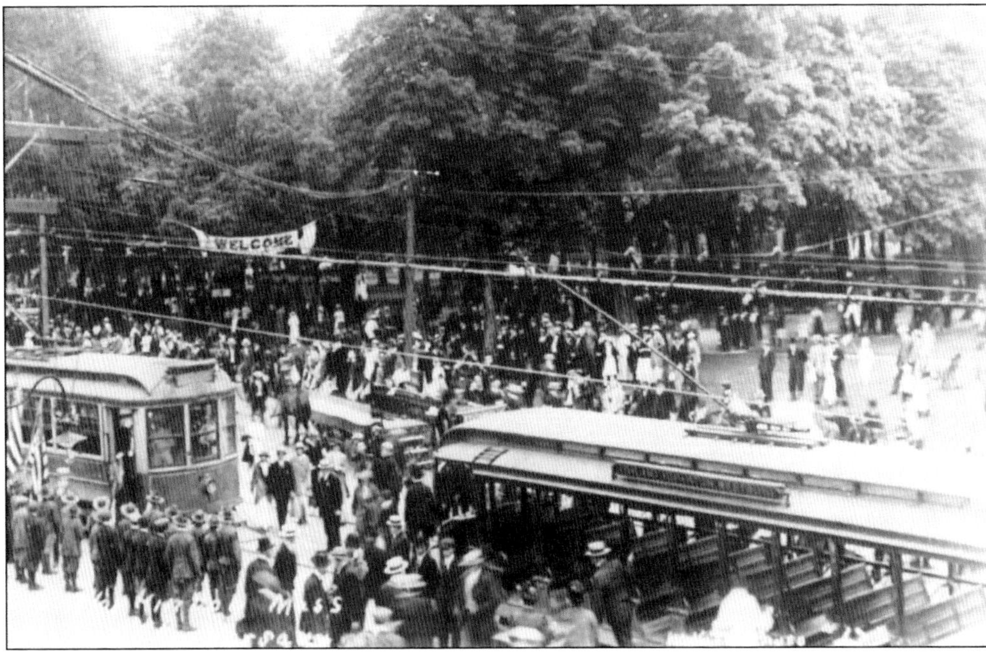

An open car, No. 12B, and a closed car were photographed on Main Street at the town common in 1915.

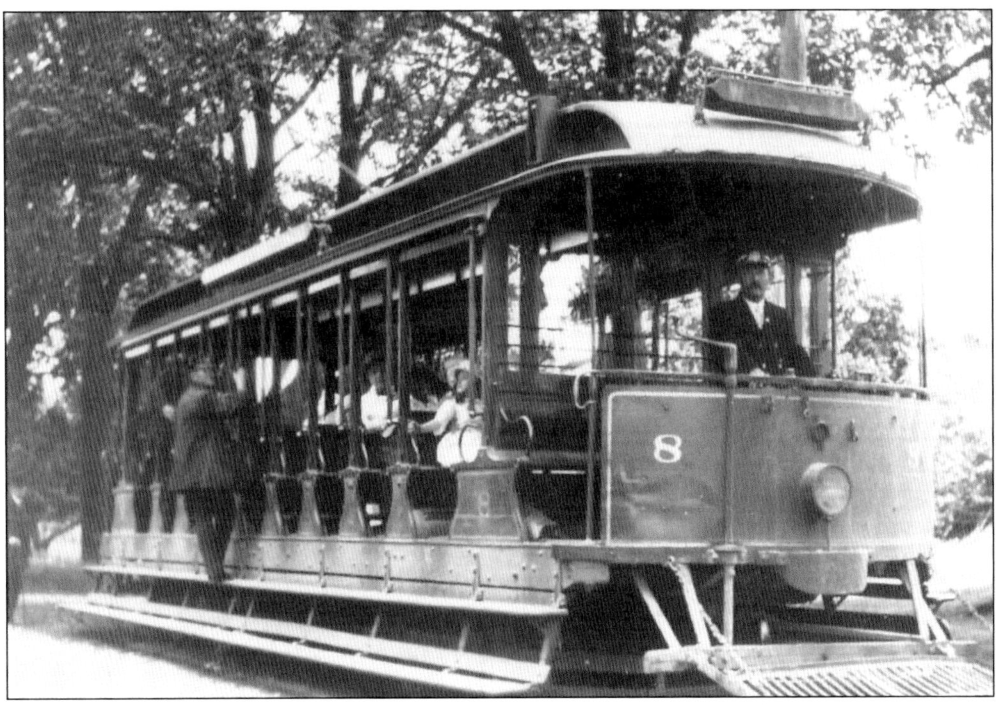

Here is the No. 8 trolley car on Main Street at the town common around 1915.

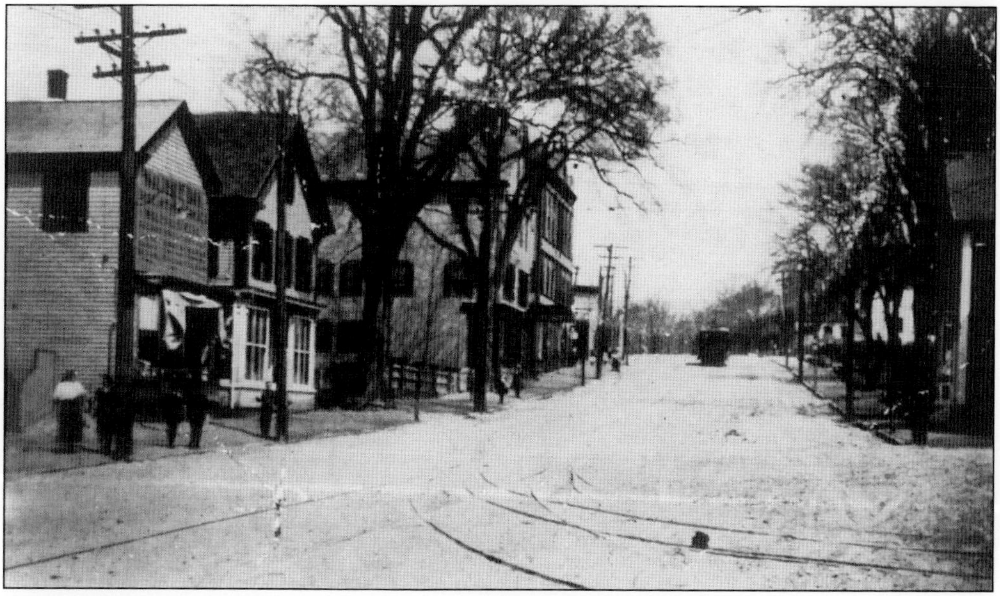

Looking east in the 1920s, one can see the trolley tracks on Main Street near the car barn.

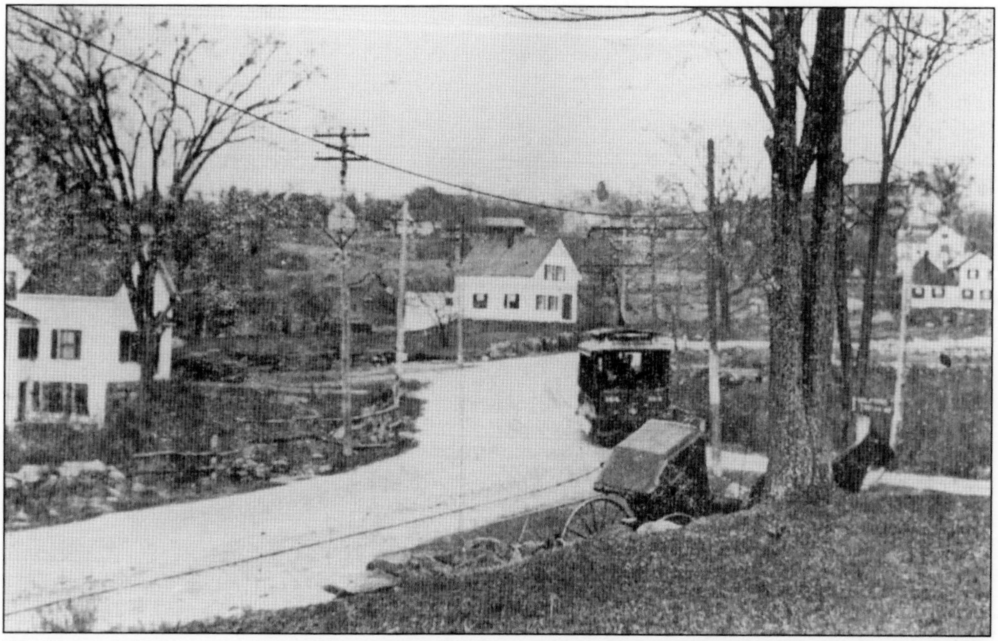

This image shows an open trolley car at the Poseyville section of Hopkinton on Wood Street in the early 1900s.

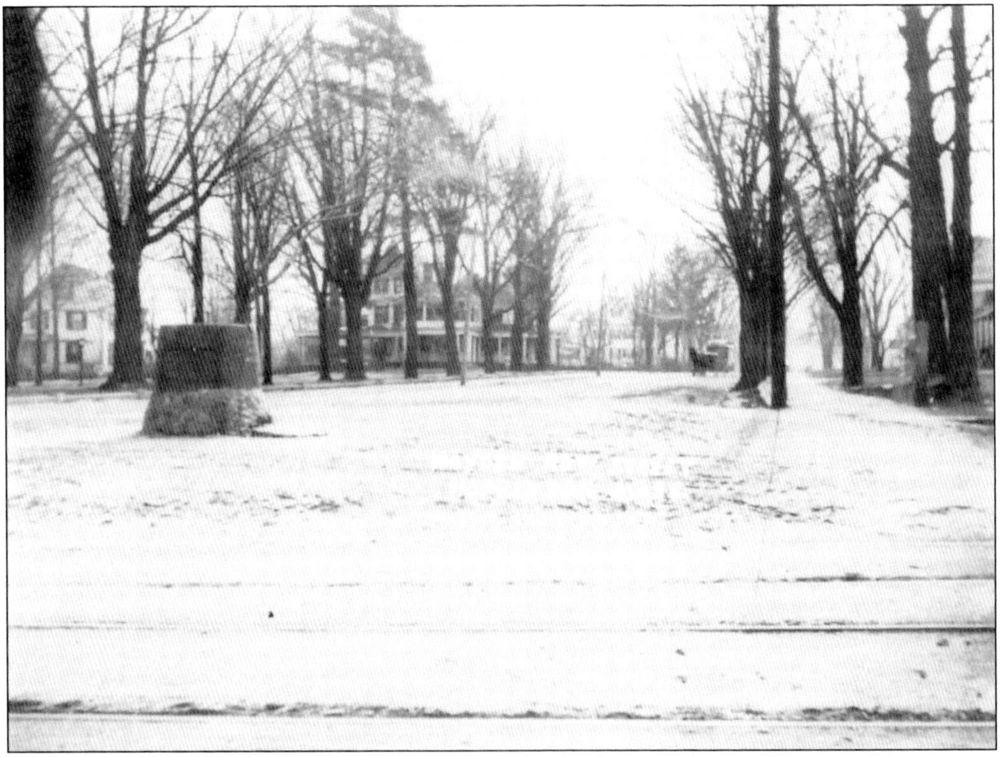

In this 1920s image of Hayden Rowe Street looking south is another trolley car. This watering trough is at the intersection of Hayden Rowe Street and Main Street.

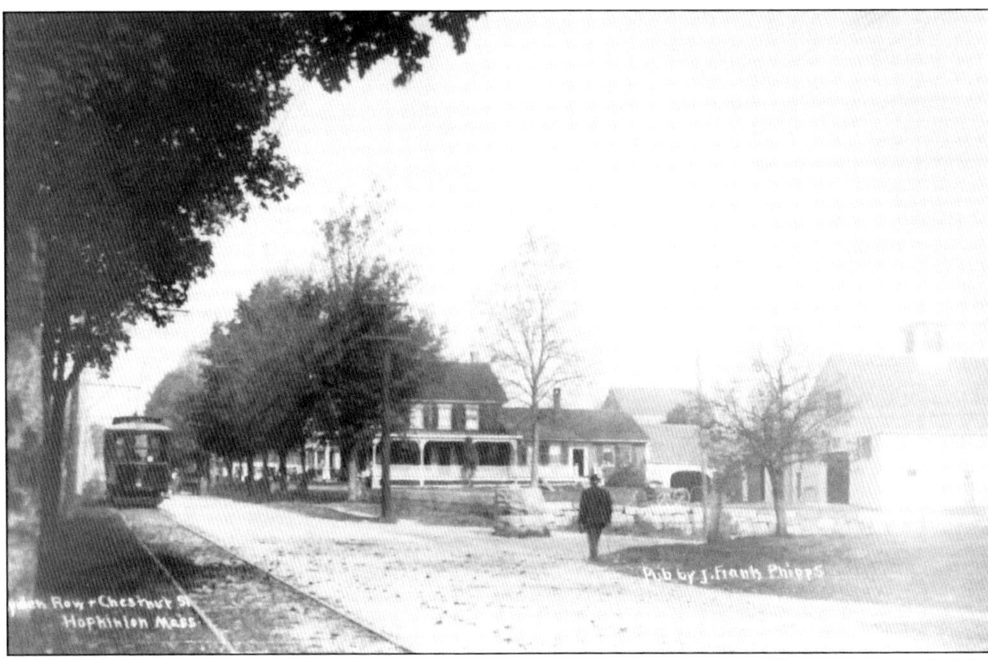

This trolley, shown in the 1920s, is stopping on Hayden Rowe Street (looking north). The watering trough is at the intersection of Hayden Rowe and Chestnut Streets.

Ten

Parting Views

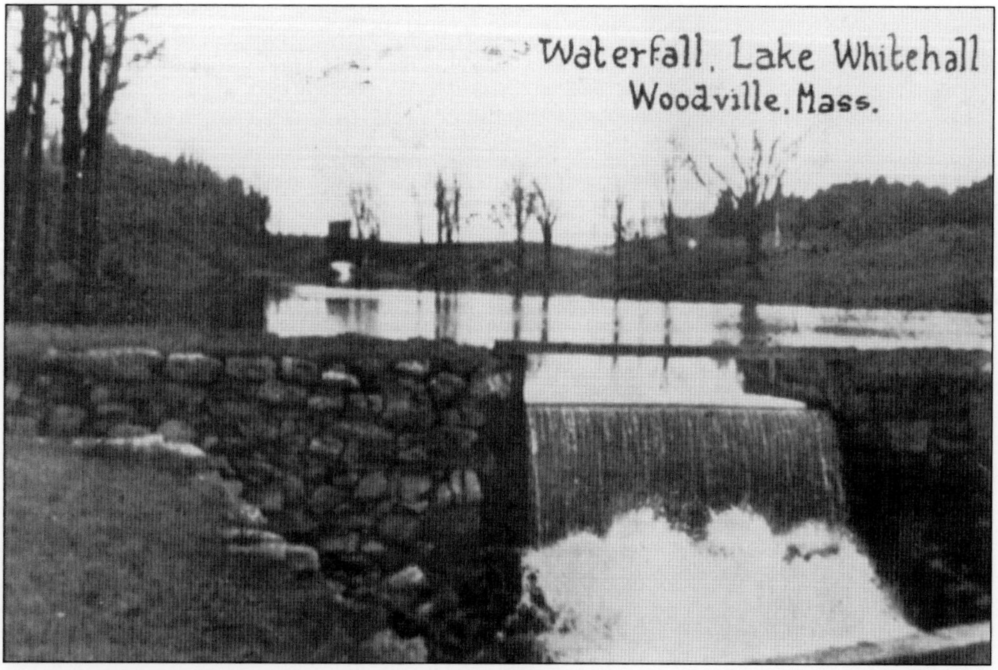

The stone dam and waterfall are shown at Lake Whitehall near Wood Street in 1916.

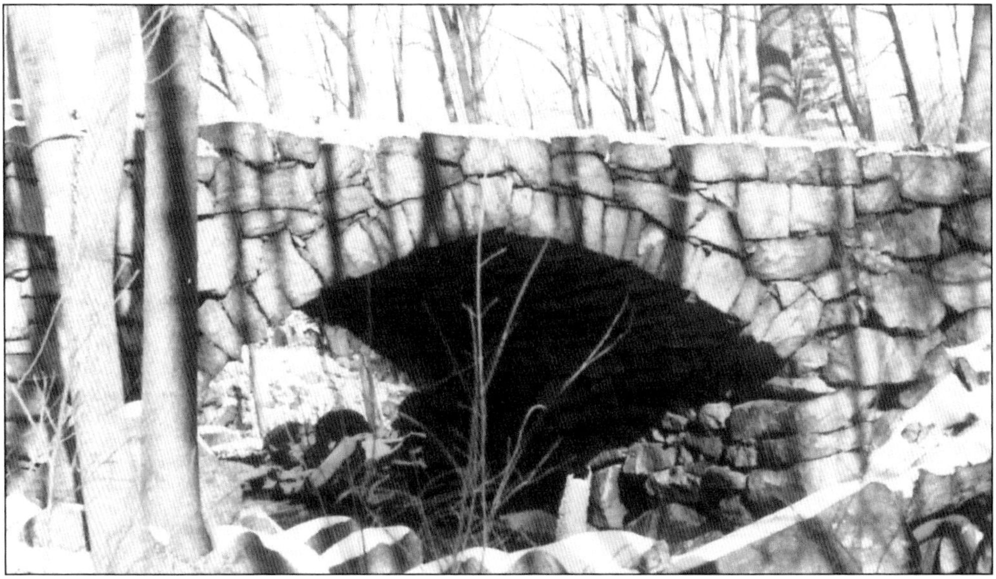

Here, an arched stone bridge spans Sudbury River near the Southboro town line. The road from Hopkinton to Southboro once crossed the Sudbury River on top of this bridge. Although the bridge is not in use today, it is still located there across the river.

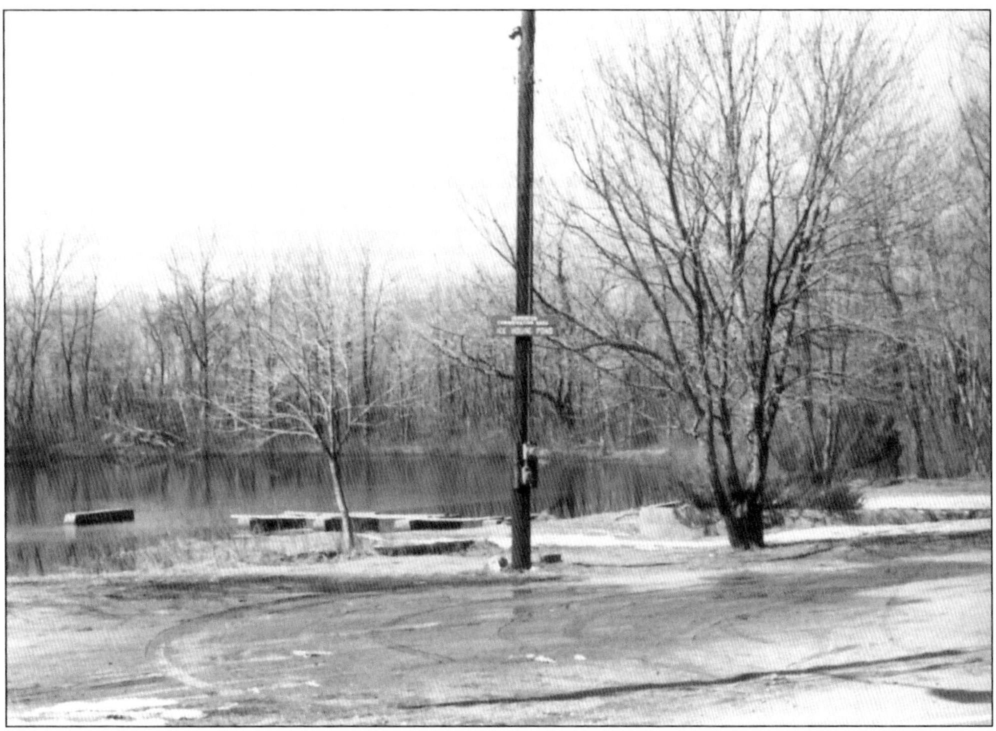

Ice House Pond lies along West Main Street. Note the concrete piers left over from the operation of an icehouse.

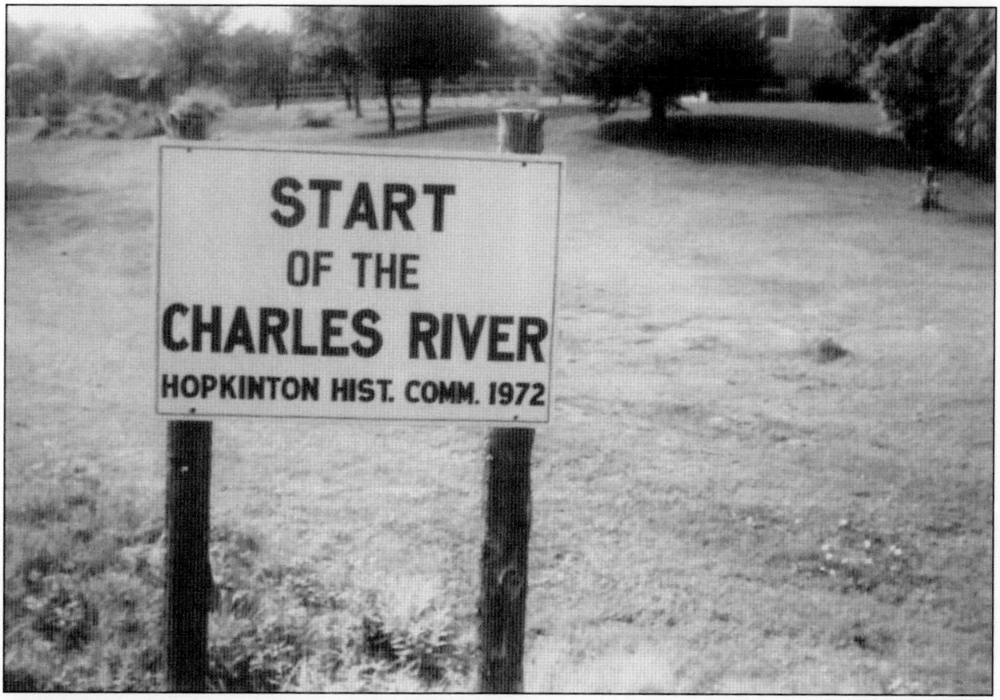

The sign designating the source of the Charles River on Hayden Rowe Street was photographed in 1972.

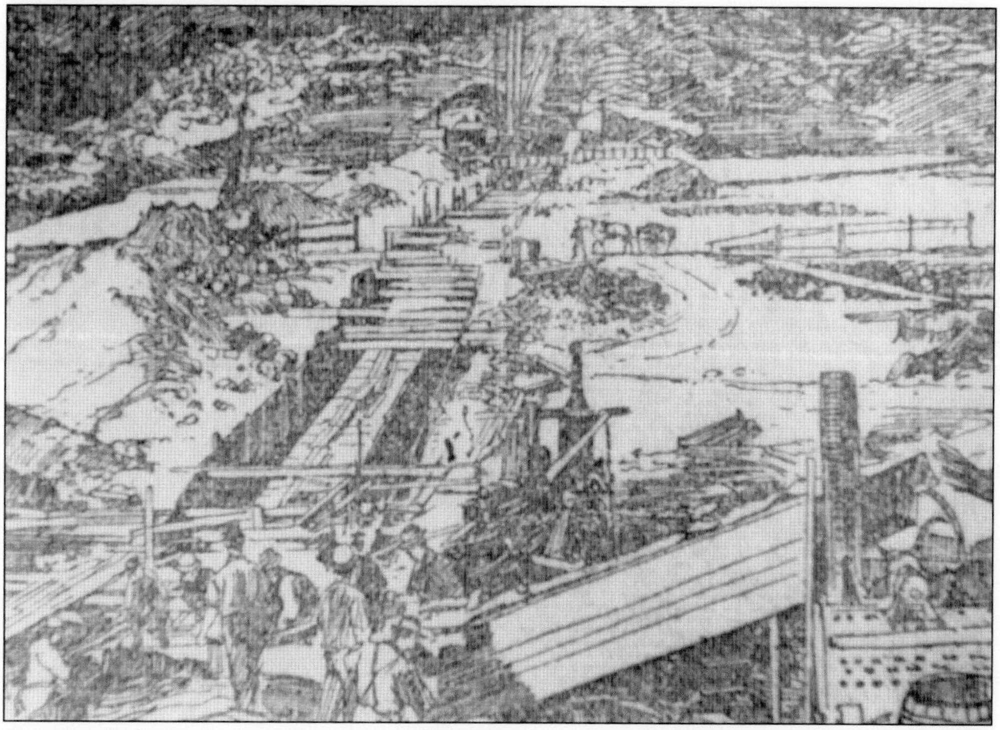

This sketch shows the large dam that was being built across Indian Brook to form the Hopkinton Reservoir in 1890.

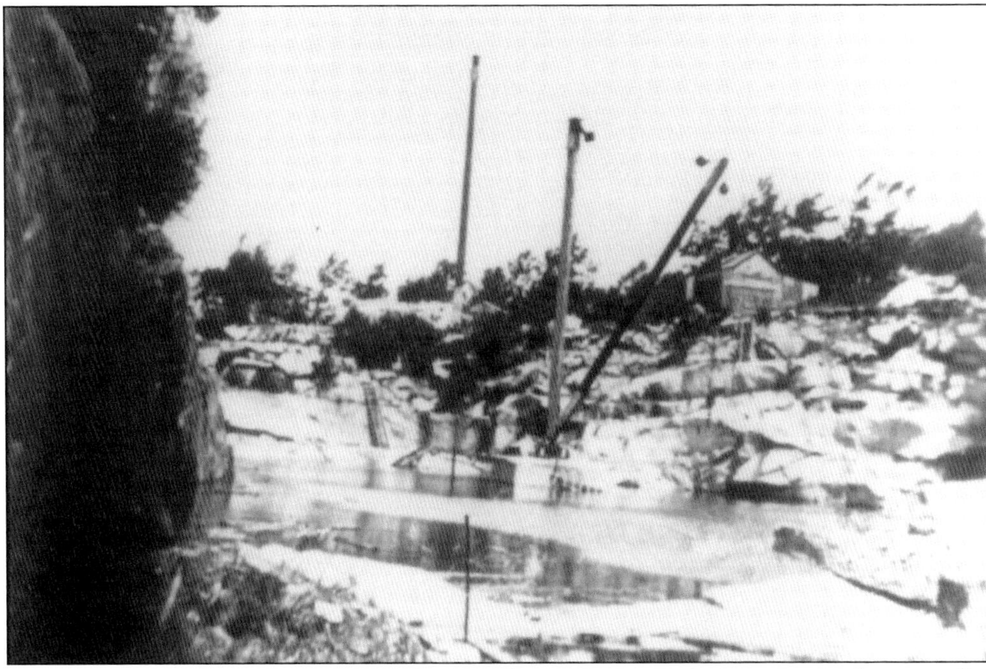

The Norcross granite quarry was located on Lumber Street in 1905. At one time, this was called the Maguire Quarry.

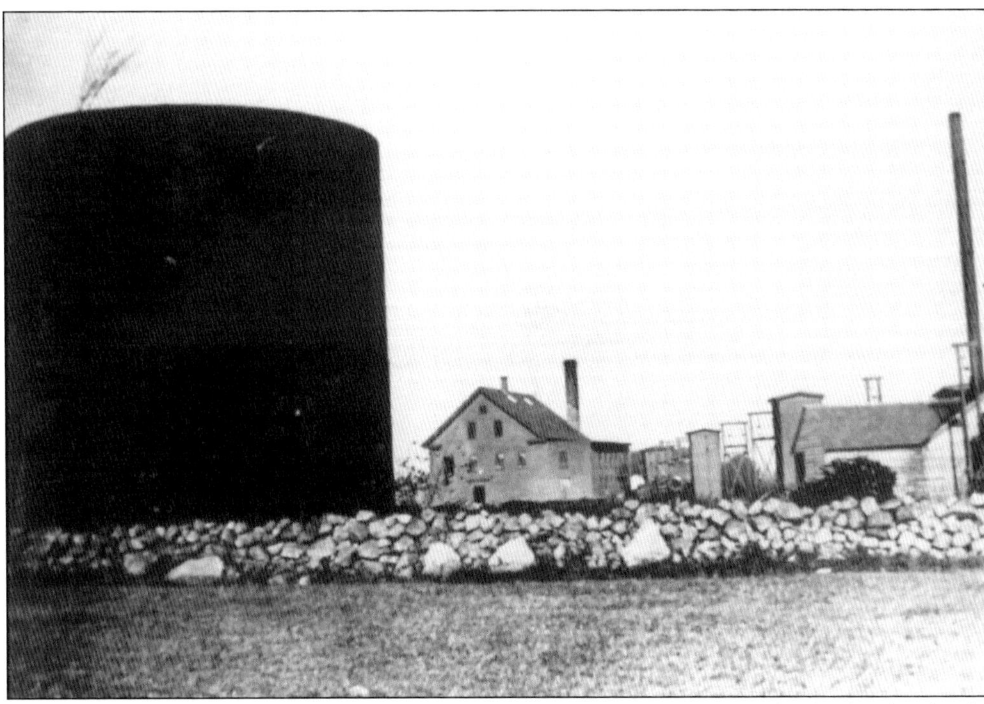

In 1900 the town's water station was on Grove Street near the present-day high school. The buildings are gone, but the old well remains.

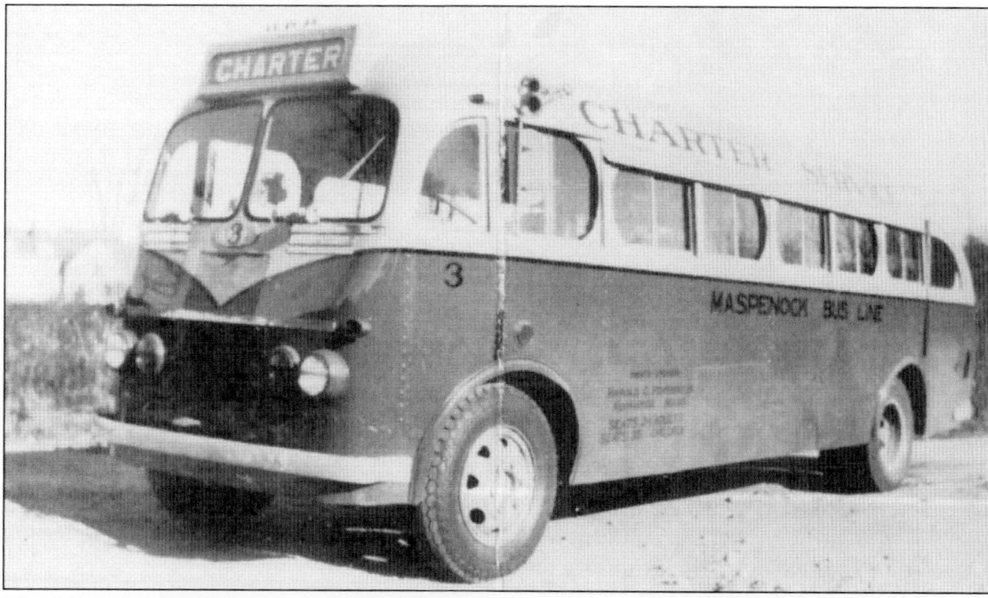

The Maspenock Bus Line was owned by Don Hitchings and Harold Penthany, and the bus operated between downtown Hopkinton and points on Lake Maspenock from 1947 to 1948.

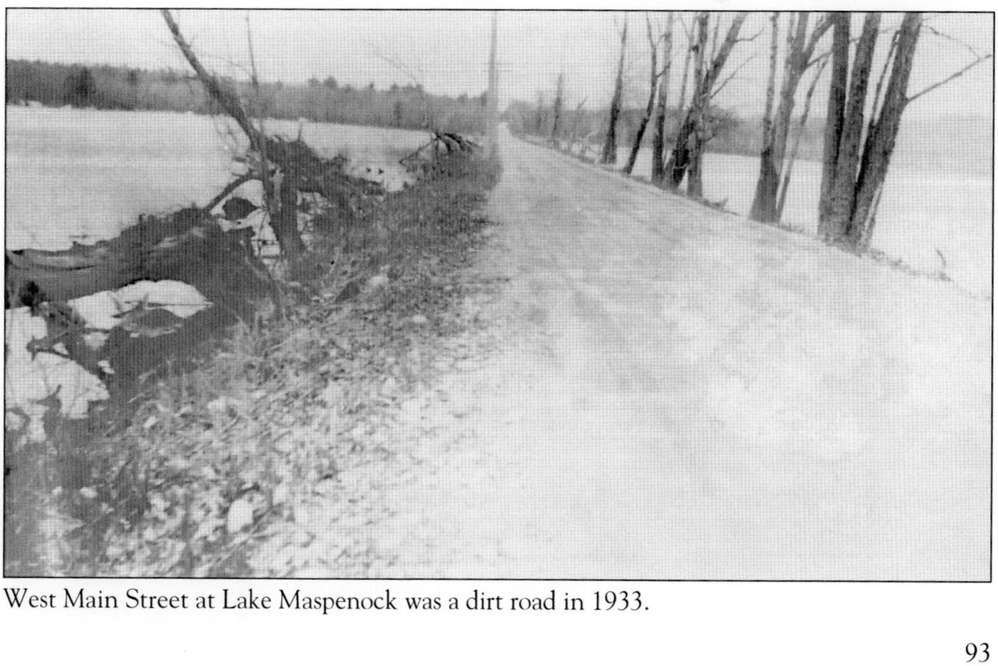

West Main Street at Lake Maspenock was a dirt road in 1933.

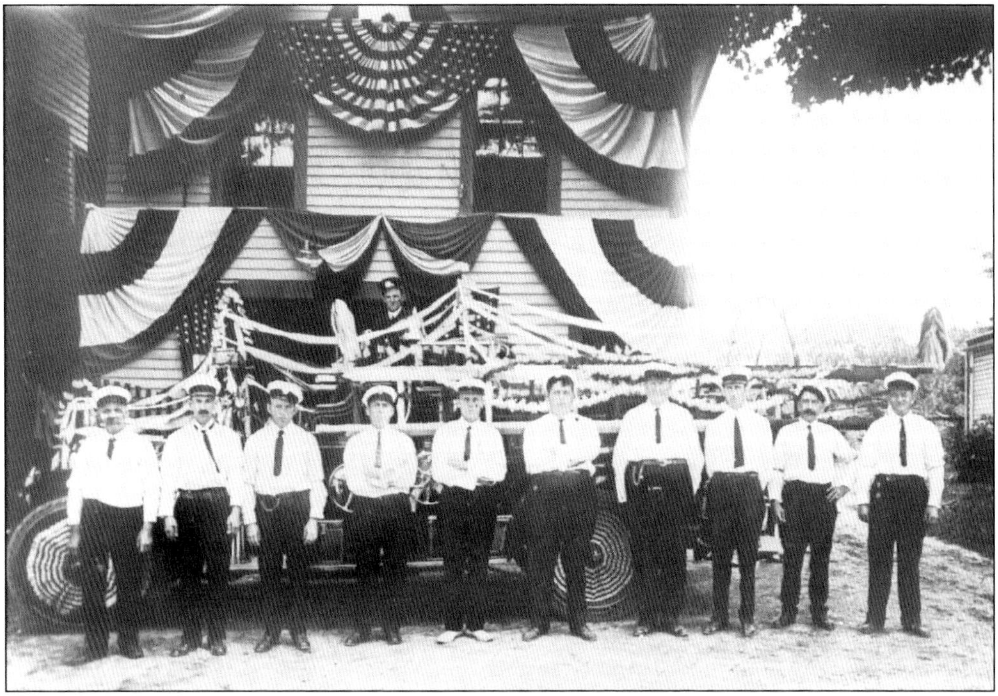

Firemen are shown in front of No. 1 fire station on Main Street in the 1940s.

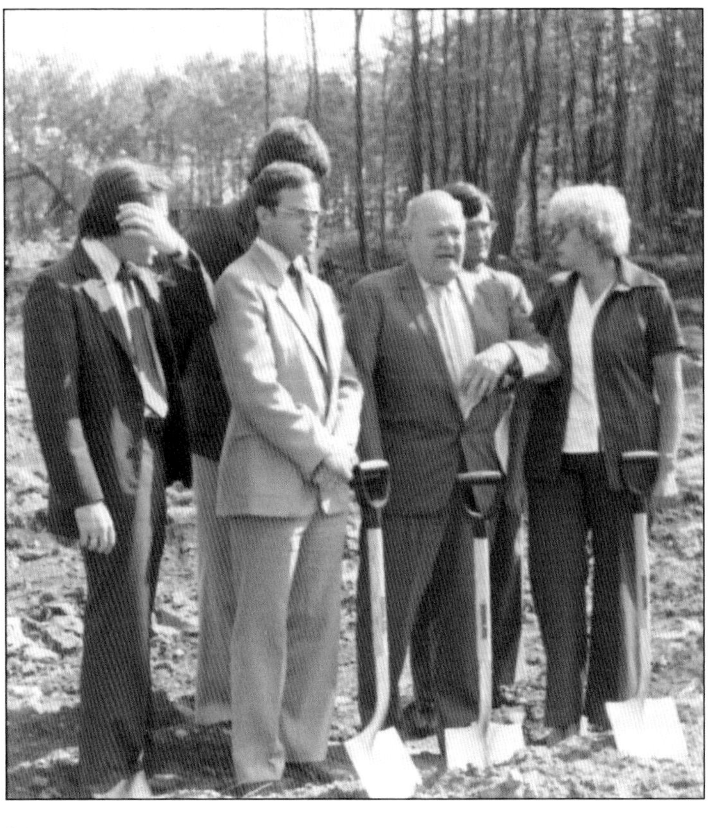

Members of the board of selectmen break ground for the new Hopkinton Office & Research Park on South Street. In the front row, from left to right, are John Hinckley Jr., Alverie Paradis, and Sallyann MacIntosh.

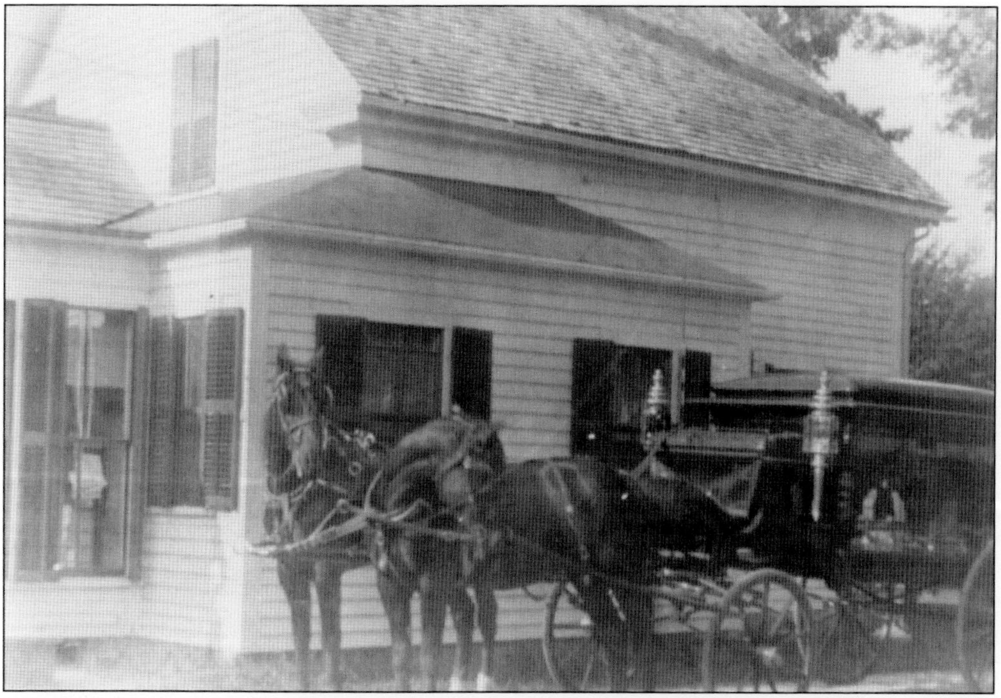

Thomas Callanan's horse-drawn hearse is shown on Hayden Rowe Street in 1890.

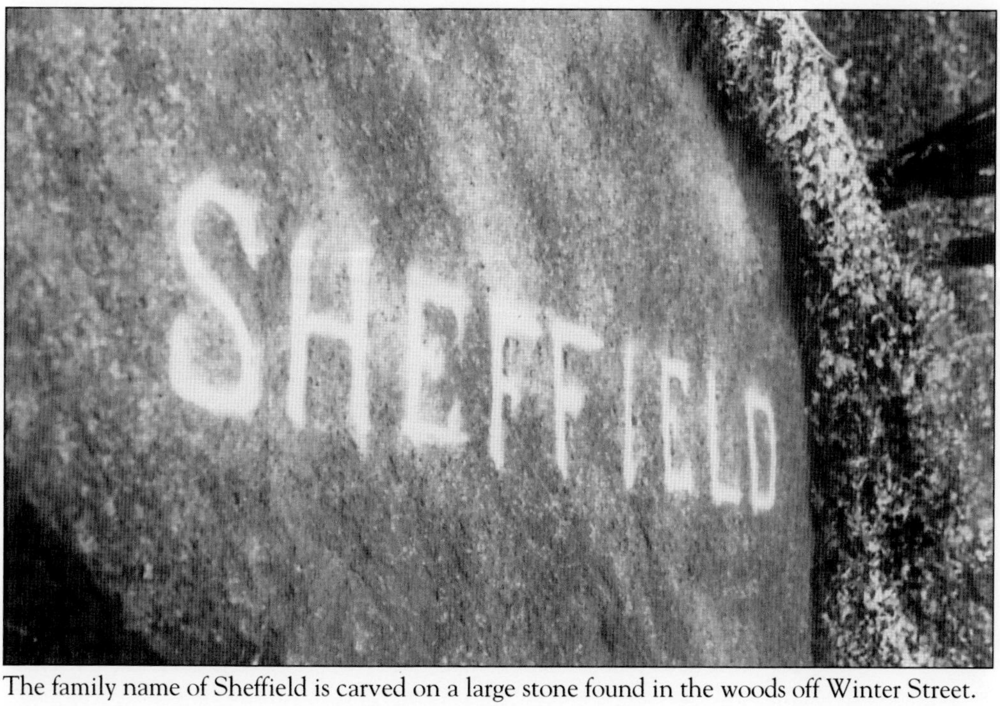

The family name of Sheffield is carved on a large stone found in the woods off Winter Street.

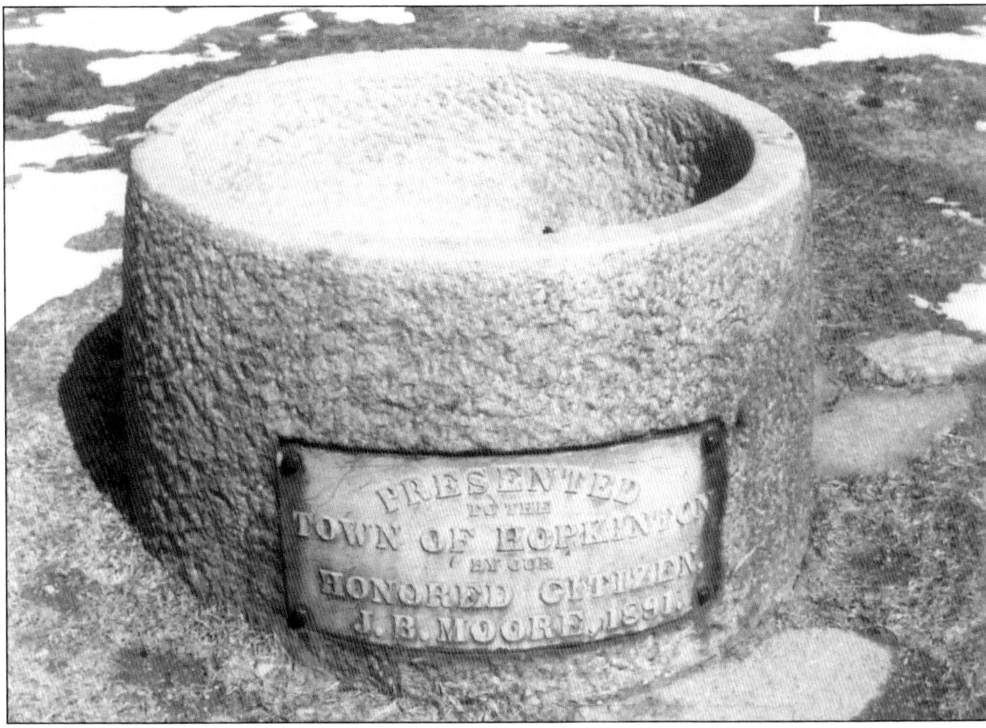

This watering trough is now preserved outside the high school. It was a gift to the Town in 1891 from J.B. Moore.

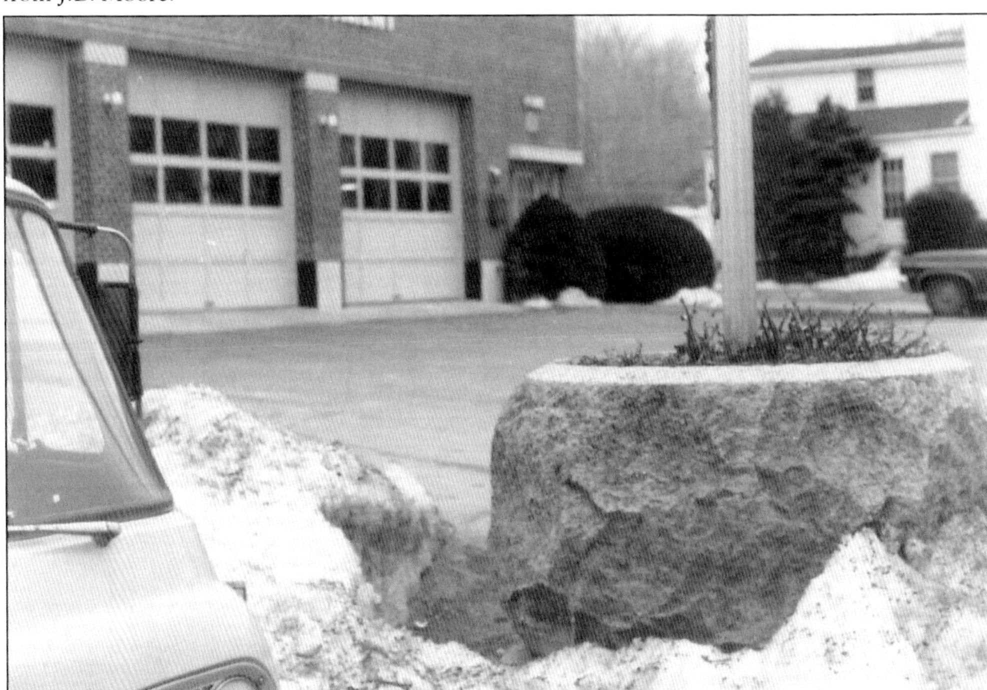

At least three watering troughs were located in Hopkinton. This one is believed to have been at the corner of Chestnut and Hayden Rowe Streets. It is now located at the central fire station.